A ***WESTERN HORSEMAN*** B LIBRARY PROGRAM

Trail Riding

WITHDRAWN

A Comprehensive Guide
to Enjoying Your Horse Outdoors

Written By Janine M. Wilder

Edited by Kathy Swan
Photography by Janine & Jim Wilder

Trail Riding

Published by
WESTERN HORSEMAN® magazine
2112 Montgomery Street
PO Box 470725
Fort Worth, TX 76147-0725

www.westernhorseman.com

Design, Typography, and Production
Western Horseman
Fort Worth, Texas

Cover photos by
Jim Wilder

Printing
Branch Smith
Fort Worth, Texas

©2005 *by* **Western Horseman**
a registered trademark of
Morris Communications Corporation
725 Broad Street
Augusta, GA 30901

All rights reserved
Manufactured in the United States of America

First Printing: December 2005

ISBN 0-911647-775

CONTENTS

FOREWORD

In the 1850s, there were a lot of things you packed into your saddlebags or the wagon before setting off to cross the North American wilderness. A gun and an ax were obvious necessities. Yet many pioneers were just as adamant about keeping a copy of *The Prairie Traveler*, written by Captain Randolph Marcy, close at hand. Next to the family Bible, it was considered an absolute necessity for anyone planning to venture through the hazards of transcontinental travel.

Though Marcy became a brigadier general in the United States Army, he made his reputation as one of America's early experts on frontier travel after tracing the Red River to its source. Soldier, trailblazer and mapmaker, Marcy conducted five major expeditions across the wilderness now known as the American West, then submitted a series of reports to the War Office describing the country, its vast resources and the hazards involved in crossing it. Those original reports formed the basis for the legendary frontiersman's encyclopedic work on frontier life and travel. The book was packed with practical suggestions for travelers, and Marcy also offered advice on the various trails crossing the continent.

The calendar might have moved on a bit from the days of Captain Marcy but the requirements of modern horsemen and women haven't changed in many respects. Like our equestrian forebears, we still long to ride toward the horizon on a good horse. But we too require expert advice on how to travel, as well as needing to know where the trails run.

Luckily for us, this new millennium has provided us with a 21st century trailblazer, only this equestrian pioneer's name is Janine Wilder.

If you set out to find a book that revealed the secrets, wisdom and pleasures associated with the trail riding experience, then look no farther. This book is it.

Janine Wilder has ridden more trails and acquired more knowledge associated with this part of the equestrian endeavor than a whole posse of the so-called "experts." A quiet woman, devoted to her horses and her husband, Janine made the bold decision to sell the family home and hit the trail full-time in the 1990s. Thousands of miles later, Janine and Jim Wilder, along with their trusty horses, Max and Smoke, are still riding the range.

During the course of their journeys, Janine was determined to master all the aspects of the trail riding experience. Her book includes all the experiences and skills that only a trail-wise veteran could bring to light.

But *Trail Riding* has more than just "school smarts." The remarkable author has literally ridden everywhere. Name an obscure trail in North Carolina, this talented writer will tell you a story. Bring up some backcountry track in Wyoming that only the old elk hunters know, Janine trotted down that road a long time ago and knows a thousand more just like it.

I think old Captain Marcy would agree with me. When Janine Wilder talks about trail riding, that's the voice of experience!

CuChullaine O'Reilly F.R.G.S.
*CuChullaine O'Reilly is a founding member of The Long Riders' Guild, the world's first international association of equestrian explorers, and author of **Khyber Knights** and **The Long Riders Anthology**.*

DEDICATION

This book is dedicated to Max Smith and his late wife, Gloria. This special couple took us under their wing and taught us what trail riding is all about. Without their help, we might never have developed our full potential as trail riders.

ACKNOWLEDGEMENTS

I'm very thankful to *Western Horseman*, especially book editor Kathy Swan, and all the wonderful staff for their expertise in producing this book.

I want to thank my fantastic husband, Jim, who went far beyond the call of duty to make sure that I was safe and sound while we experienced our adventures in trail riding. Without his support I couldn't have gotten back on a horse and, therefore, would've never been able to write this book or learn what special talents our two horses have.

A very special thank-you goes to retired Maj. Gen. Lynn Stevens and his wife, Lynette, along with Larry and Johnni Bailey, who never declined to go riding with us locally or around the country. They cheerfully endured any weather condition, terrain and my constant picture-taking, which is a sign of true friendship.

To all our trail riding friends and to the thousands of trail riders we've met and ridden with all over this incredible country, we thank you all for showing us your favorite trails, letting us show you our favorite trails and most importantly, sharing yourselves and your love for trail riding.

PREFACE

I've been at Janine's side through our many years of trail riding and traveling with horses. At the end of each ride, it always astonishes me how many beautiful photographs and observations she's made. It's hard to believe that I was on the same trail ride. I guess I was busy running my mouth while she was taking in the picturesque scenery or analyzing the characteristics and habits of other riders and their horses. When someone asks which trail we should take or which direction we should go, they'd better listen to Janine. She has an uncanny ability to remember trails and landmarks that most of us fail to observe. But, of course, fellow trail riders could do as I've done so many times when I chose my way rather than hers. Soon, I'd find myself eating crow.

Janine's trail riding career nearly came to an abrupt end before it even got started in a very serious riding accident on her first horse. A horse trader sold us the older mare, which by all reasonable standards, should've been retired. Unfortunately, we relied on the wrong people to help us get started. The horse tripped on a gravel road, causing Janine serious injuries. She had broken bones and numerous internal injuries, and it looked liked her equestrian career had come to an end. That was just one of the many challenges in her life that she has had to overcome. Her injuries could've discouraged and perhaps even have been career-ending for most novice riders, but not Janine. The event made her more resolute than ever to not only overcome her fears of riding but also to dig in her heels and muster up the courage and strength to become the highly acclaimed expert in the trail riding community that she is today.

Janine has taken her writing ability and her scientific and analytical background and put these skills to work for her in the sport of trail riding. She's been able to advance trail riding techniques to a new level. She accomplished this by not only studying other riders in the field but also by taking a hands-on approach in developing trail horses and riders.

Janine has ridden in 49 states (48 of them on her horse Max), which gives her a wealth of experience to draw upon. Her book offers this knowledge and includes other important material such as tips on how to find the right trail horse; techniques for navigating typical trail obstacles, such as water, deadfall and many other hazards; ways to deal with wild and domesticated animal encounters on the trail and hassle-free, problem-minimizing methods for traveling with horses. Also, one of the most important aspects of developing as a competent trail rider is to learn to understand your horse and his natural instincts as he acquires his trail savvy. On these pages, Janine helps you identify and work with those instincts.

I'm sure that the combination of useful trail riding and travel information and the many real-life adventures that Janine has experienced will enrich all who read her book. I think that you'll come away with renewed interest and enthusiasm for trail riding and traveling with your horse. Perhaps you'll plan your first trail adventure or take Janine's lead and ride the backcountry wilderness you've always wanted to do. Whatever your interest, I hope you enjoy reading her book as much as I did.

In loving admiration to my wonderful partner and friend.

Jim Wilder

INTRODUCTION

Lying on our bed in the camper is a small decorative pillow that reads "Live to Ride – Ride to Live". It's been a part of my camping décor every since I found it in a small shop in the Black Hills of South Dakota on one of our many riding trips to the area. The horseshoe-clad words say it all. I believe life is too short – riding my horse is my life and I intend to ride as much as I possibly can for the rest of it.

Although I didn't start riding horses until my late thirties, I have certainly made up for lost time. My only equine discipline has been trail riding; nothing has captured my heart as the tens of thousands of trail miles, the companionship of my husband Jim and the talents of the trail horse.

Years ago when Jim and I first started riding horses, we looked everywhere for information on how to trail ride, but to no avail. Experience and our good friends, Max and Gloria Smith, were our only sources for education. I approached the activity as I did any of those in my career in the field of engineering research and development. I spent my time thinking about the how-to aspects and observing the behavior of my horse and that of others. It wasn't long before I discovered a new world. Not knowing anything about horses or riding, my learning curve was fast and furious.

I can't tell you how many hours I've watched my horse Max and Jim's horse Smoke out on the trail. I'd observe other horses, too, and listen to what other riders had to say, then analyze it. When I came to some kind of conclusion, I'd test it on myself, while trail riding, of course.

There came a point in time when Jim and I wanted to see the whole country from the backs of our horses. Our kids were grown and on their own so it was a good time to sell our home, put all of our belongings into storage and hit the road.

We lived in a 36-foot motor home as we traveled from state to state and trail to trail. I drove a pickup truck with the horse trailer so we could get back to the trail heads that were off the beaten path. I can't begin to tell you what an experience those years on the road were. We learned so much about ourselves, this wonderful country we live in and, of course, trail riding.

After more than 20 years of traveling to 48 states, Hawaii and Mexico's Yucatan jungle, trail riding has simply become our lifestyle. We ride as many as eight to ten hours a day, five or more days a week. Rain or shine.

My passion for trail riding and traveling with horses is equaled only by my desire to write about my adventures. I want to share the knowledge I've gained over the years in hopes other trail riders can learn from my experiences and mistakes, so they can improve their skills and perhaps fulfill their dreams. I hope the miles of trails I've traveled can be of help to you and other trail riders. And, most of all, I hope you have a safe and happy trail experience.

Janine Wilder

1 TRAIL RIDING: AN OVERVIEW

Trail riding can be a leisure hobby or a serious sport.

Emerging as one of America's most popular equine sports, trail riding encompasses everything from the Sunday afternoon pleasure trail ride to an adventurous, cross-country wilderness trek. What was once an activity that gained its direction from other riding disciplines has now developed into a discipline in its own right. Note that while this book specifically addresses recreational trail riding, endurance riding is a recognized Olympic equestrian discipline and competitive trail riding and trail trials are gaining in popularity nationwide. So, it's safe to say that trail riding includes much more than the casual ride through the woods. In fact, it's grown into a sport that takes as much, if not more, preparation, training and skill as any equine discipline.

One of trail riding's greatest attractions is that it provides the horseman opportunities not available in any of the other horse communities. Horse and rider delve into a world that offers the outdoors at its finest, experiences of a lifetime and nature as real as it can get.

There's no better way to enjoy your horse than in his natural environment, where his innate abilities and instincts are at their best.

The trail horse's image has certainly changed over the years from that of a reject from other disciplines or breeds to one of an athlete, capable of tackling challenging obstacles and traversing difficult terrain, all the while making wise choices to ensure his and his rider's safety. No longer do you hear the trail rider say, "Well, he's just a trail horse." Instead, he boasts, "My horse is a trail horse!"

Trail riders can see and enjoy a whole new world from the back of a horse – a world arena riders never get to experience.

Trail horses must be athletes to negotiate all types of terrain.

Types of Trail Riders

The term "trail rider" means different things to different people. Trail riders come from all walks of life, and many enjoy other riding disciplines, as well. They range from the horsemen who enjoy a pleasant ride on a sunny afternoon to the die-hard riders who spend every day they possibly can riding, in all climates, anywhere and everywhere possible.

I've categorized different types of riders for the purpose of making distinctions. As you read the descriptions, you might see yourself in one type, or as a combination of two or more.

Pleasure Rider:

A pleasure rider enjoys his horse by taking leisurely rides on nearby trails and roads. He might even trailer short distances to seek out different and inviting trails. Riding with friends on a beautiful sunny day is common. Generally, the trails have easy to moderate footing.

The pleasure rider typically uses a horse that's very well-behaved and seasoned to the trail. He normally doesn't ride on complicated or difficult terrain; his goal is to take an

A leisurely pleasure ride with an equine partner can also include a canine friend.

uncomplicated and enjoyable ride. A pleasure rider's average riding schedule is a few days a week for a couple of hours at a time.

Trail Trainer:

Trail trainers are riders who like to incorporate horse training with their trail riding. These riders aren't necessarily professionals who make their living as horse trainers. They're usually trail riders who enjoy the challenge of training their own horses, and the trail provides natural obstacles for them to work. Many professional horse trainers use the trail as an excellent tool in their training program, as well; however, I don't consider them included in this category.

The trail trainer accomplishes two things on the trail. First is to give his horse experience while using the opportunity as a training lesson, and second is to enjoy the great outdoors. This type of trail riding places the emphasis on training. A trail trainer's riding schedule usually averages a few days a week for a couple of hours at a time.

Note: If you're a trail trainer, make sure that the others riding with you are aware of what you're doing and don't mind the distractions.

Social Rider:

Social riders are the largest group of riders in the trail riding community. They enjoy camping with their buddies, along with other local groups, and/or on organized trail rides. Their emphasis is on being social with other horse people while riding trails. Their riding and camping, for the most part, is done in a

Trail trainers look for opportunities to school their horses on the trail.

group setting. Time-wise, they devote one to two weekends a month on their favorite activity.

Organized trail rides are a great way to enjoy riding horses and engage in camaraderie of like-minded people. The food on these rides is usually catered or a potluck. Either way it's delicious and an important part of the social gathering. Folks have been known to attend organized rides where they've been so involved with the social aspects that their horses never left their stalls or pens. Now that's being social!

Social riders also like to travel in groups to their destination. This can be a great way to travel so long as everyone is compatible. Most folks are used to their own schedules and habits; therefore, a few might get irritated with others who don't fall into their routine. You also want to keep in mind the more people, the more rigs and the more horses in the group, the more problems that might arise.

Advanced Trail Rider/Wilderness Rider:

Advanced or wilderness trail riders are horsemen who have a real infatuation for adventurous riding, especially in remote areas. It's the primary focus of their equestrian life. These trail riders place their emphasis on exploring different trails, in various terrains and in most weather conditions. They generally love traveling to all areas of the country to ride their horses, which can easily develop into their life's passion.

Traveling with horses for the sole purpose of riding has truly grown in popularity over the years. Serious trail riders have their own riding dreams, whether they wish to ride in the mountains, on an ocean beach or in the high desert. The thought of exploring what's over the next hill or around the next bend is thrilling to them. People who are best suited for this kind of riding are very adaptable, adventurous and physically fit. They must be in order to ride for many hours, over long distances and difficult terrain. These riders can spend anywhere from a few days to a week or more per trip and might go on several extended trips a year.

Riding your horse in different places is a wonderful way to see the country. However, you must be cognizant of your riding skills and your horse's abilities. Also, advance planning and preparation are key to making this type of trail riding an enjoyable experience and lack of it can turn into a nightmare.

Riding with friends makes the activity all the more enjoyable.

Advanced trail riders don't shy away from difficult terrain.

Extreme trail riders will "bushwhack" off-trail to get where they want to go.

At designated check points, veterinarians carefully examine endurance horses to make sure they are fit to continue.

PHOTO BY KATHY SWAN

Extreme Trail Riders:

Extreme trail riders are the smallest group in the trail riding community. An extreme rider loves to bushwhack or ride off-trail as he explores the backcountry. He'll ride most anywhere and under nearly all conditions. When it comes to horsemanship, he has to be skilled in the art of communication with his horse. His horse must trust him completely, but the rider, too, must listen to his horse and exercise good judgment in negotiating tough terrain. If not, he takes the chance of getting himself and his horse hurt.

Competitive Trail Rider:

Many trail riders enjoy competing on their horses. It gives them a sense of accomplishment to show off their and their horses' skills in a competitive environment. There are three main types of activity: North American Trail Ride Conference, American Endurance Ride Conference and trail trials.

The AERC sanctions races, generally from 50 to 150 miles, and the horse and rider duo with the fastest time is the winner, providing a veterinarian judge assesses the horse's condition as sound and healthy at the end of the race.

The NATRC offers one- to three-day rides over a prescribed course of 15 to 90 miles, which the contestants must complete in a specified time period. However, competitive trail rides are not races. Horses and riders are evaluated individually, with the

LIFE ON THE TRAIL

Max Doesn't Rock 'n Roll

Organized trail rides can be fun if you like social activity, but have you ever wondered if your horse enjoys them? I believe most horses like to get out on the trail as much as we do. However, I have reason to question whether they enjoy such night-time activities as noisy musical entertainment.

One night, we were at our campsite with our friends Max and Gloria Smith, enjoying a relaxing conversation about the day's trail ride. As we heard the band start to play, we realized we were late for the evening's entertainment. We quickly got up and were heading for the cafeteria, where the band was playing, when we noticed my horse, Max, acting strangely. In fact, he was acting very strangely for this usually well-behaved and quiet gelding. While tethered on a highline with his trail-mate, Smoke, Max would suddenly twirl around, stomp his front feet, kick out frantically and even rear. I did everything I could think of to quiet him. I tried walking him, treating him to grass, talking to him, moving him around, but

nothing seemed to help. After observing him for a while, we realized that his strange behavior was in direct correlation to the high-pitched notes the rock-n-roll band was playing. If the music was truly the cause of his behavior, what could we do for the next three hours while the band played?

After thinking about it for a few minutes, our friend Max (not to be confused with my horse Max) suggested putting wadded-up paper towels in his ears to block out the sound of the band. Well, we all had a big laugh, but after a few more minutes of watching my horse's antics, we decided to try it. After all, we had nothing to lose. The first time we plugged his ears, Max shook his head and paper towel balls went flying through the air. Once again we placed them in his ears (being careful not to push them too far) and immediately he stopped his bizarre behavior and within five minutes he was resting comfortably. We had no more problems with music after that. I guess Max just doesn't like rock n' roll.

Riding the backcountry is a great way for couples to connect with one another.

winners earning the most points. Horses are judged on soundness, condition, manners and way of going and riders on equitation and horse care.

Trail trials, most of which are held on the West Coast, are judged pleasure rides in which riders negotiate obstacles over a marked course. There are no time requirements, and the contestants are judged against a standard for each obstacle. The obstacles aren't necessarily natural, such as the typical ditch, downed timber or stream a trail rider might encounter. Some can be quite hair-raising (balloons, umbrellas, llamas, etc.), testing the metal of the most experienced trail horse.

Competitive trail riders, especially the NATRC and AERC varieties, usually ride several times a week from a couple of hours to half a day, in order to condition their horses. Trail trialers don't have to worry as much about the conditioning aspect.

A New and Popular Lifestyle

The increasingly popular sport of trail riding is breaking new ground for riders and trail groups alike, nationwide. The evidence can be found in the sheer number of horse motels, overnight stabling and public trail facilities that have sprung up all over the country, helping the trail rider to enjoy the outdoors whether he ventures near or far from home.

Although these places help tremendously, trail riding involves much more than where to hang your halter along the way. How-to information for the trail user has been very sparse, particularly in the area of traveling with your horse and riding trails in different areas of the country. My hope is that this book changes all that.

To me over the years, trail riding has been living life to the fullest. It's exploring a world I never knew existed, and I've discovered a part of myself that might never have had the opportunity to surface. Given a chance, trail riding can become your life, too.

2 CHOOSING THE RIGHT TRAIL HORSE

Trail riding is all the more fun with the right equine partner.

Having the right horse for the right job is of the utmost importance. This is especially true for the trail horse that's used extensively for riding various terrains, maneuvering obstacles and dealing with different altitudes, climates and the strenuous rigors of traveling. As for the everyday trail/pleasure horse, many equestrians proclaim that any

A couple of trail-savvy Paints make trail riding for this couple a pleasure.

horse can make a good trail horse. For the most part, that might be true. However, for the advanced trail rider, there's far more to that equation than meets the eye. As you consider your trail riding plans, evaluate your current and future needs carefully. The wrong choice in a trail partner could be uncomfortable at best and dangerous at worst.

The Search is On

There definitely are desirable characteristics a good trail horse should possess. He should be athletic, smart and sensible. He should also have lots of endurance, be easygoing and have plenty of trail savvy. It's important to have a horse that'll keep both of you out of trouble as much as possible. The chances of getting hurt while on or around horses are extremely high even under the best of circumstances. Therefore, it's not wise to ride a horse that could raise the odds in favor of a disaster. Such a horse is usually high-strung, poorly trained, badly conformed and/or has a combination of these undesirable traits.

When you're ready to choose a suitable trail horse, consider the following. Will this horse be used for trail riding only or will he need other qualities for other disciplines? If you're a pleasure rider but want to participate in other events, your needs for a trail horse will be far different than someone who wants a horse exclusively for advanced trail riding. For example, if you also want to compete in western pleasure or hunter-under-saddle classes, then your prospect must also be handsome and talented enough to pass the muster in the show ring, at the same time he's confident to venture outside an arena. However, for advanced trail riding, a serious trail mount doesn't need a pedigree, good looks or specialized training, but he does require a good attitude, durable conformation and a willingness to explore trails.

In choosing the horse you're going to spend many hours on, it's extremely important that you be very selective. Don't be persuaded by friends, relatives, horse breeders or anyone else for that matter, on the kind of horse you need. If you feel you don't know enough about trail riding to make an educated decision, find someone who trail rides extensively and ask his or her opinion. However, ultimately the decision should be yours and yours alone and only after you've given a lot of thought to what you're looking for in a trail horse.

Breed popularity by regions and riding circles is common. It's not unusual for a group of friends to all have the same breed of horse. Of course, it might be easier to ride with a group of folks who have the same breed. However, don't buy a horse just because you've heard it's the best trail breed or you want to "fit" into the group.

Buying a horse just for its color, popularity or breed isn't a great idea. However, if you have a choice between two great trail horses, the deciding factor could be the color or breed. Keep in mind that any horse has the potential to seriously injure or even kill you, so don't take the selection process lightly. Make your choice by using your head, not your heart. Your life might depend on it.

Picking a Prospect

Choose a horse with the intention of keeping it. That way you won't be inclined to think of just trying out a horse, and, if it doesn't work out, buying another one. By doing that, you end up wasting a lot of valuable time out on the trail. The more time you spend on the

A horse that's easy to work with makes life a lot simpler. This horse behaves well for the farrier.

trail, the more trail-savvy both of you'll become. But if you're constantly changing horses, you can't possibly develop your full trail expertise.

At the other end of the spectrum, some riders keep horses that'll never have the ability to be great trail horses. Many buy horses without putting a lot of thought into what they need. After having their horses for a while, they become attached to them. At that point they tend to overlook all the faults because they've bonded with their horses and couldn't possibly part with them. There are problems, however, that might be beyond your expertise and should be tackled only by a professional.

On the other hand, don't be so quick to judge and let a good horse slip through your fingers because of a few little quirks. There are little annoyances that can be corrected without a lot of hoopla. After all, the term "sweat under the saddle blanket" says a lot about the trail horse. You might be surprised by what experience can do for a horse and for you, as a matter of fact. Therefore, spend the extra time looking for the right horse. It'll be worth it in the long run. The longer you ride the horse on the trail, the better trail horse he'll become.

It's best to start with a horse that has already learned the fundamentals. In other words, he should be well broke. He should steer, stop and back well. It's important for him to stand still for mounting and while tied in the trailer or anywhere else that he's expected to stand quietly. A horse on the move can create many dangerous situations. Other plusses include a horse that's easy to

A good trail horse should stand tied quietly anywhere.

Group riding usually brings out any crankiness a horse might have and can pose a danger to the others. The riders in this group have horses that get along fine.

shoe, stands well for the veterinarian and loads and unloads from the trailer with a minimum of problems.

I don't recommend buying a green-broke horse that needs to learn the basics, unless you're a trail trainer and you enjoy it. For the most part, however, fundamentals should be addressed with ground work at home, not on the trail.

The following are physical characteristics and mental traits you should consider in your search for the perfect trail partner.

Gender

There are great trail horses of all sexes, but geldings are the gender of choice. They're generally calm and their attitude, for the most part, is more predictable. Also, they typically get along with other horses better than stallions and mares do.

Some mares have quiet dispositions and good attitudes, which make them great trail prospects. However, some become temperamental, cantankerous and even aggressive during their heat cycles. You might have to pay more attention to a mare around other horses than you would a gelding.

Stallions, even ones thought to be non-threatening, might pose a danger to other riders, as well as horses. They could, with no provocation, become aggressive toward a gelding or too attracted to a mare, especially if

she's in heat. There have been numerous stories about stallions mounting mares, with riders on their backs! If you want to travel with your stallion cross-country, you should be aware that they might not be permitted at a lot of facilities.

Disposition

The horse you choose to be your trail partner should be well-behaved and have a first-rate disposition. It's always a pleasure to be around a horse that enjoys people, and one

Having a horse that genuinely enjoys being around people is a plus.

that appears to take pleasure in what he's doing. It's especially gratifying when you're traveling and riding new trails.

Getting along with other horses is also a must for a trail horse, whether they're in the next stall or out on the trail. An aggressive horse can be a major problem. Kicking or biting at other horses is very dangerous.

You don't want a horse that's harebrained nor do you want a deadhead. It's not fun spending the day trying to keep up with the other riders, or trying to control a horse that's jumping around and acting crazy. When you're out on a new trail you don't want to deal with problems that should've been handled long before you got there. It's hard enough to keep your attention on the trail and its obstacles; you don't need to be worried about a horse that won't stand still while you're trying to mount or one who tries to run over you while you're leading him over an obstacle. Your time and efforts are better served on other priorities, and, besides, it's no fun to have to deal with a difficult horse.

Conformation

When it comes to conformation, your trail horse should have the best you can find. You aren't looking for a show-quality equine, but you are looking for a top-quality trail horse.

The better the conformation your horse has, the fewer problems he'll have and the more you'll enjoy the ride. The horse's build contributes to his sure-footedness, his ride, his balance and the overall trail experience. If you aren't familiar with what to look for in good conformation, have your vet assess your prospective purchase. It's especially important to have a sound horse if you intend to spend lots of hours in the saddle on all kinds of terrain.

Generally speaking, a well-conformed horse is proportional throughout his body. For example, his front end isn't bigger than his hind end and vice-versa, nor does he have short legs and a long torso. A strong and athletic equine body has shoulder and hindquarter angles that match one another, a short back and a long underline. This type of conformation allows a horse to use himself effectively.

The horse doesn't have to sport a beautiful head, but his eyes should be set wide on the sides of his head to allow him good peripheral vision. The neck should be of medium length, neither too long, nor too short, and the throatlatch

Outstanding trail horses can be found among all breeds. When shopping for one, make sure the individual has sound conformation. As an example, this Quarter Horse has many excellent conformational traits: wide-set eyes, strong back, good withers, deep heart girth, long underline, well-developed hindquarters, straight legs, good bone and solid hoofs.

should be clean, so the horse can easily flex at the poll in response to rein pressure.

The horse should have a large heart girth and well-sprung rib cage for lung capacity and a solid back – one that boasts a good set of withers to stabilize a saddle. The hindquarters should be strong and tie down into a well-developed set of gaskins on the horse's legs. All four legs should have good bone, clean joints and stand as square and straight as possible.

Horse's hoofs are extremely important, as the old saying goes "no hoof, no horse." Look for a horse with strong healthy feet; otherwise they might not hold up over the years and miles of trails. If you aren't sure what to look for, have your vet or farrier look at the horse's feet for you.

Horses's hoofs come in all shapes and sizes, but, in general, they should match the size of the horse. In other words, you don't want small feet on a large horse. A nice, round shape is preferable, as are wide open heels, a well-developed frog and some concavity to the sole. A horse with contracted heels is a candidate for unsoundness and flat feet predispose a horse to bruising. Thick, not thin, walls and soles are crucial for a horse traversing difficult terrain. Only a farrier can really assess the quality of the hoof horn and its depth. You could have your farrier look at the prospect's hoofs, much like you'd have your veterinarian perform a pre-purchase exam on any horse you consider.

Hoof color isn't important. There's an old wife's tale about white hoofs being soft or inferior to black ones, but there's nothing to that myth. It simply means the hoof is lacking in pigment. Most horses with white leg markings that extend down to the coronary band have corresponding white hoofs. Those with dark legs have black hoofs. Striped or banded hoofs, such as those on Appaloosas, are thought to be of high quality.

Sure-footed

Being sure-footed is essential for the trail horse, and it can mean all the difference in your safety. It's very possible your horse might be more sure-footed in different circumstances and on different terrain. However, you don't and can't know these things until you're actually out on the trail and experience this.

You can't teach a horse to be sure-footed. However, there are a few things you can look for in a trail prospect that'll help you deter-

You can check to see if a horse "caps" his feet by riding him over soft ground, such as sand.

mine if the horse has the potential to be sure-footed in most situations. One important factor is his foot placement. For a real eye-opener about a horse's surefootedness, take him out for a ride where you can see the imprint of his hoofs on the ground, such as in sand, clay or soft dirt. After you ride him at a walk, look at the hoof prints on the ground. You want to see if his back feet "cap" his front feet, which means his back feet cover the prints of his front feet. The closer he does this, the better it is. It's been my experience, watching thousands of horses, that those who cap their steps are more sure-footed on the trail than those who don't. Try this at various speeds and see if there's any difference. It's not unusual to see a horse cap his steps at one pace and not at others.

If he places his back feet automatically where his front feet were, especially when navigating obstacles such as fallen trees, tree roots and rocks, he has a much better chance of clearing that obstacle. It only makes sense that if his front feet were placed clear of the object and he places his hind foot in the same spot, he will be clear. After many years of riding

Gaited horse riders having fun gaiting through a mountain meadow.

with mule riders, many would tell me that this is one of the abilities that make the mule so sure-footed.

A horse might cap his step at a fast gait, but at a walk his steps might be farther apart. That might mean that he's great in a fast gait on flat land. To test this further, take him to a hilly area, or where there are lots of downed trees to see how he tracks there. Use caution as you proceed through any obstacles. If you find the horse is sure-footed only at a fast gait on flat land and not in rougher country, then you'll certainly know where the best place to ride him will be.

Another clue to a horse's agility on the trail is how he raises his legs while traveling over obstacles. A horse should have a nice way of going over hurdles on the trail; his stride should look smooth and effortless as he lifts his feet high enough to get over any barrier. If he continually hits his toe on every little rock, twig, or bump in the trail, you might want to re-evaluate his performance.

Along with being sure-footed, a good trail horse always watches where he's going. It doesn't matter if he's the first horse, in the middle or the very last horse on the trail, he pays attention to what he's doing. He doesn't go down the trail with his nose on the ground all the time, but his nose isn't in the air either. He makes his way down the trail in a safe manner, looking down when the need arises to check out his footing.

Gaited Horses

Ever wonder if you need a gaited horse for your trail riding pleasure? There are a lot of great trail horses out there that aren't gaited. However, the older you get, the more you might appreciate a smoother ride. If you spend a lot of time on the trail you'll want to be as comfortable as possible.

In addition to comfort, long strides on a horse are an advantage if you want to cover a lot of territory. Most gaited breeds are blessed with being long-strided. Their conformation is structured in such a way that the prints of their hind hoofs often overlap the prints of their front hoofs, thus giving them a longer stride than the average non-gaited horse. When walking or gaiting, they cover more ground, naturally.

Horse Height

Riders have individual preferences about the size of the horses they enjoy riding. In general, though, the horse should be proportionate to the rider's height and weight. A tall, hefty man usually is more comfortable – and looks better – on a tall, stout horse.

However, on the trail, a short horse can be an asset for several reasons. First, he's much easier to mount. As we age, most of us lose some agility, and it isn't as easy as it used to be to spring up on a 16-hand horse. On some rides, you might need to dismount and remount several times, and there might not always be a log to stand on, or a ditch to walk the horse down into.

Second, the shorter the horse, the closer he – and you – are to the ground, which you might appreciate a great deal should you fall off.

Last, riding a shorter horse means it's easier to maneuver under low-hanging tree branches, rock ledges and such things. On some difficult trails you still might have to dismount, but having a shorter horse might mean you don't have to unsaddle him too.

Size can become an issue for such things as saddling and mounting.

Endurance

If you know your trail riding treks are going to be long and frequent, you'll want a horse that has good endurance, although this quality is hard to discover when you look at the trail prospect. What you want is a horse who can go all day, every day and then go some more. You can build any horse's endurance over time, but some horses just have natural staying power. This innate ability can certainly be to your advantage. This isn't to say you should ride only Arabians, a breed well known for their natural endurance capabilities. They excel at 50- and 100-mile endurance races, but that isn't what this book is about. For recreational trail riding, most properly conditioned horses have sufficient stamina to get you there and back. Breeds such as Quarter Horses, Appaloosas, Morgans, Paints and any of the gaited breeds can make exceptional trail riding mounts.

Spooky

Horses react differently to new surroundings, but there are behaviors to look for in a trail mount that might help minimize spooking problems. When looking for that special trail horse, check to see how he responds to a potential problem. You might try opening a noisy, yellow slicker in front of the horse to assess his response. Do so while unmounted, of course. What does the horse do if it startles him? Does he show fear, but stand in place as he checks out the situation or does he take off for the hills? Of course, the preferred horse is the one who stands his ground.

There are laid-back horses that just don't let much get to them, but I wouldn't necessarily call these guys spook-proof. Do you want a horse that didn't care about his surroundings? Horses have to be attentive on the trail. You want a horse that's aware of what's going on in his environment. There needs to be a balance.

A new environment, a new trail or something new on a familiar trail should get your horse's attention. You want him to look at it, listen to it and even smell it. From time to time, even the best of trail horses will become startled by something, but you don't want a horse that jumps at every little thing. You want one that acknowledges things on the trail. If he looks but continues to move on, that's the best reaction.

A horse that pays attention to his surroundings is more likely to be aware of what's going on around him long before he actually encounters it. His ears should move around as

These horses weren't expecting a motor bike out on the trail, but they handle it well. Their riders allow them time to check out the "monster."

if he's trying to hear something. If he takes the time to look in a certain direction, there just might be something there that has caught his attention. Alertness is a great asset for a trail horse. There are times while riding out on the trail that something will make me jump but my horse goes on like nothing happened. That's because he was already aware of it. Smart horse!

Also, realize that horses kept to the same environment, riding the same or similar trails, become very tolerant of familiar situations and, therefore, don't show much excitement

LIFE ON THE TRAIL

Cheating Death

I remember so vividly the words of one of our favorite saddle pals, Gloria. Upon arrival back at camp after a full day's ride she would always comment, "Whew, cheated death again," as her foot slid from the stirrup to the ground. She made it a point not to make the statement until she was safely off her mule. There's a lot to be said for that statement. Many times have those very words ran through my mind as I returned from a ride in which there could have been unpleasant consequences with someone in our riding group.

I know from my own experience after tens of thousand of miles of riding that I took a chance every time I got into the saddle. However, I also know that without a doubt, that even on our worst days, my chances of getting back to camp safe and sound were in my favor because I had the right horse.

LIFE ON THE TRAIL

Easy – Coming and Going

I'm not sure I really knew what an easy-keeper was until we'd been on the road for several years. Now I know that without a doubt, our horses are easy-keepers. Our horses, Max and Smoke, have been on the road in a horse trailer for well over 100,000 miles. They've been in every climate possible in the lower 48 states and at elevations from sea level to almost 13,000 feet. They've eaten hay and feed from hundreds of different sources. Their water supplies have come from big-city water systems and shallow puddles on a desert floor. The only constant in our horses' diet over the years has been change. Therefore, I believe that I can safely say, "Our horses are easy keepers."

over any small changes. On the other hand, if you constantly ride on new trails and in new areas of the country, things will be different, which can make riding your horse a little tricky. However, in time and with experience, your seasoned trail horse should learn to accept new situations with confidence.

Our horses, Max and Smoke, are always aware of their surroundings whether they're on the trail, in the pasture, or in the trailer. In fact, the minute the trailer comes to a halt and we open the trailer door, our horses are looking, listening, and smelling. As they're unloaded, their ears are up and moving around, listening to the immediate sounds, sniffing the air and looking around at their surroundings.

Some horses are just simply jumpy, almost as if they're just looking for something to spook about. This isn't a terrible thing if you can tolerate it. However, if the horse dumps you every

time he thinks he sees a monster, he's not a good trail prospect. Some horses can overcome some of their frivolity with experience on the trail, but others are just that way.

Easy Keepers

Traveling to different regions of the country is a lot easier with "easy keeper" – a horse that's content to eat whatever kind of hay or feed is available, drink the water and isn't picky about his overnight facilities.

It's almost impossible to buy the same brand of feed or type of hay wherever you go. Even the most popular brands aren't available everywhere. It's impractical, if not impossible, to take all the feed you need on extensive trips. If your horse is an easy keeper, your problems with feed and hay are at a minimum.

Water varies from one location to another. An easy keeper is able to adjust to whatever you present to him. However, this can be easily handled with the common practice of adding a flavoring to the water. Start adding the flavoring, such as molasses, before you leave home to give your horse time to adjust to the flavor. I've never had to use anything, but I've even heard of folks using Kool-aid.

Horses that have a history of colicking aren't considered easy keepers. Colic is a serious problem, and one you don't want to deal with while en route or out on the trail.

It's best if your horse is accustomed to various forms of confinement, especially before going out for the first time. If your horse is normally stalled, you should familiarize him with other forms, such as high-lining or picketing. Stalls aren't readily available at most horse camps.

LIFE ON THE TRAIL

Non-fatal, but Embarrassing, Attraction

There are horses and mules that are so attached to their stable mates that they can't be kept apart under any circumstances.

One time while on a break during an organized trail ride, ladies and gentlemen were directed to different parts of the forest for a little privacy. A friend was riding a mule that belonged to her boyfriend. As we rode off to our designated part of the woods, the mule started braying for her buddy. We continued on with the rest of the girls and went on with our business. However, Kate, the mule, became more and more frantic as every second passed.

About the time my friend's jeans approached her knees, the mule had reached the breaking point and took off to the place where she'd last seen her equine compadre. My friend had thought it'd be best to hold the mule rather than tie her to a tree. She didn't want to let go of the reins, and the mule dragged her back to the reunion. Unfortunately, my friend was unable to retrieve her jeans, which were now around her ankles. The mule finally found her pal and stopped – right in the middle of the men who'd returned to the gathering place to wait for us. What more can I say! (Names have been omitted in order to protect the embarrassed.)

Two horses that get along well make trail riding all the more fun and safe.

Partners

If you plan to do a lot of riding with someone else, such as your spouse or another trail buddy, then it's important for your horses to get along. It's absolutely no fun to have a couple of horses fighting and picking on each other all the time. Plus, it's not safe for you to be in the middle of the fray.

At the other end of the spectrum are the barn buddies. Stable mates can often become so attached they can't let their buddy out of their sight. They can become totally out of control when they're separated. Such a horse might do stupid things, such as jumping over an object or off the trail, that can be detrimental to the rider. Horses have been known to knock other horses and their riders out of the way as they go crashing through a group. If you're going to be riding a horse like this on the trail, you should work out the problem before attempting to ride with others.

The right trail horse isn't a particular breed, color or gender. The right horse is the one that does what you want it to do and performs in a safe manner so you and he can have a great ride, time after time.

3 TIPS ON BUYING A TRAIL HORSE

If he lives in a pasture, notice how the trail prospect gets along with other horses.

Buying a new horse isn't an everyday experience for most of us and evaluating a potential trail prospect is different than assessing a horse for another discipline. Keep in mind what characteristics make a good trail horse, as discussed in the previous chapter on choosing a trail horse. Formulate your questions before you arrive at the seller's ranch/farm and before you see the trail prospect. It's important you don't lose your focus while viewing your choices. It's easy to get carried away with all the beautiful and talented mounts from which you can choose. Just remember, you're picking the best horse for the trail, not a show or arena horse, for the most part.

Questions and Answers

Make an appointment to see the trail prospect in his home environment. That can be either at the seller's ranch/farm or it can be at a boarding stable, wherever the horse lives. While making the arrangements, ask that the horse be left in his usual surroundings. If he lives out in a pasture with other horses, ask the owner not to catch him before your arrival. This'll give you the chance to see how he interacts with his pasture mates and, better yet, it'll give you the opportunity to see how easy he is to catch. His interaction with pasture mates will give you a clue as to how he'll get along with trail mates.

If he lives in a stall or pen, make special note of how the seller catches the horse. When the seller approaches the stall door or gate, does the horse pin his ears or move to the back or both, avoiding contact? That tells you the horse has a cranky disposition and probably doesn't much care for people for some reason. This is not to say, however, that you can't overcome his dislike of humans by your actions when you get him home. Many a grouchy horse turned sweet with common horse-sense behavior on the part of people.

Also, if the horse moved to the back of the stall or pen and turned away from the seller, presenting his rear end, this is a clear sign of disrespect and lets you know where humans are on the horse's totem pole – the bottom! But again, this is something that can be improved upon with proper horse-handling skills. But be aware, that you'll have to work on this bad habit immediately, to gain the horse's respect and confidence before you ever go out on the trail.

Note: Here's the typical training technique used to address this respect problem. Flick the end of a lead rope at the horse's hindquarters, from a safe distance, of course, until the horse turns and acknowledges you. Or use a buggy or longeing whip to tap (not hit) the horse's hindquarters or the ground behind them until the horse turns to face you. Your object is to have him look at you with both eyes, giving you his full attention. However, this happens slowly and by degrees. The instant he makes even the slightest move to turn to you, stop flicking or tapping. That tells him what you want him to do. Begin again until he looks at you with one eye, then stop. Let him figure out what you're asking him to do. Then, begin flicking or tapping once more and continue until he turns around completely to face you. This could take some time. Don't frighten the horse into turning by being too aggressive; ask him to turn with your consistent flicking or tapping.

In a group, does the trail prospect ride quietly in line?

LIFE ON THE TRAIL

Don't Fence Me In

We drove up to a farm to take a look at a trail horse a man had advertised for sale. When we arrived, we couldn't help noticing a red roan horse and a mule inside an incredibly high wire fence. As we walked up to the fence with the farmer, he told us he would really like to sell the pair together. As he told the story of how these two friends were inseparable, it became clear why they were behind the eight-foot-high fence. Whew, that was a close call, because it surely wasn't a problem we were looking for. The lesson learned: Pay close attention to your sale prospect's environment and listen very carefully to what the seller has to say.

It's a good idea to insist on this catching scenario every time you approach him, whether it's out in the pasture or in his stall. Never walk up to a horse when his butt is toward you. To do so is not demanding respect at the least and dangerous at most.

Notice other important things about the horse at this time. Definitely examine his conformation, especially his legs and feet, to see if they meet with your standards. If they don't, then don't waste your time any further. Ask if it's okay to pick up the horse's feet – all of them.

Watch how the seller saddles the horse. Does the animal stand still or does he move away? Does he accept the bit well?

It's a good idea to ask the seller as many questions as you can. Even if you observed the horse earlier in the pasture, one important question is: "Does this horse get along with other horses?" It's crucial to know this, especially for a trail horse. The chances are very high that he'll be around other horses, in a stall, out on the trail, next to others in a corral, etc. His encounters with other horses will certainly be many. Of course, if he's a good trail horse in every other way, you can always make other arrangements for his overnight facilities and put a red ribbon in his tail while out on the trail. A red ribbon is a universal trail-rider's sign. It means to be careful of the horse that wears it. Don't crowd or come up on him fast.

Try to ride the prospect on different types of terrain.

Will the horse willingly lead or leave the group?

He'll kick. However, if the horse doesn't have these problems, it makes for a more pleasurable trail experience.

If you aren't a good judge of horseflesh, especially of trail horses, it might be a good idea to bring someone with you who does know what a good trail horse is all about.

The Trail Trial

Having a trial period or at least taking a few "trial" trail rides on any horse you're thinking about buying is optimum. It's best to take the horse for a week-long trial period; but if this isn't possible, perhaps you can go to the farm/stable on several occasions to ride the horse and spend some time becoming acquainted with him. Another option is to at least take the horse out for a ride, preferably away from his home. You need to get a feel for the horse's trail abilities without the distractions of his home turf.

It's important to figure out if the horse will do what you ask and expect of him. This is best done while riding with other horses. If your trial is short, you must make the best of the situation. Be aware of the horse's behavior and keep in mind what your needs are. There are very few horses that might be a perfect

LIFE ON THE TRAIL

Different Strokes for Different Folks

When we arrived at the ranch to see a new trail prospect for our 14-year-old son, a young lady was riding a horse that fit the description of the horse we'd come to see. The horse was a gorgeous chestnut and smooth as glass. The owner met us as we were getting out of our rig. We chatted as we watched this beautiful animal maneuver around the grounds.

He asked if we wanted to ride Rico. It's our policy that when we look at a new trail prospect, we always ask for the person selling the horse to ride him first. The owner quickly answered that he couldn't do that. The horse didn't care for him, he remarked, and said he was selling Rico because

every time he tried to ride Rico quickly bucked him off. He said Rico didn't respond that way to anyone else. So, he was in the market for another horse.

After Jim rode the horse and he and I had had a long discussion, we decided to take the horse. Our son, Clint, was very pleased with the horse and rode him on trails all over the country for a couple of years without any problems. Then at the age of 16, like most teenagers, his riding adventures turned to dreams of driving a car. At that point we told him the story about Rico and his bucking abilities. We all had a good laugh about it, but it certainly did teach us a lesson: Horses can react differently to different people and situations.

match for you. Evaluate the horse with regard to what you can deal with and what you can't. Some maneuvers, behaviors or habits can be changed; it's a matter of what you believe you can honestly handle yourself.

You want to feel comfortable while trail riding. It usually doesn't take long on a horse to know whether the ride's what you're looking for. If the horse isn't comfortable, then it's not likely the horse is going to make you happy when you ride him all day. If he passes the first test, you're ready to continue.

While in line with others on the trail, see how he reacts to being in front, in the middle and at the end of the line. Does he walk out when in front and does he keep up when he's in line or does he lag back or ride on top of the horse in front of him? Watch for aggressive signs such as pinning his ears back or offering to bite or kick.

There are obvious warning signs, such as rearing, bucking or throwing his head, that give you a good indication of the horse's general behavior. How does he react to objects and potential spooks? Any time the prospect displays behavior you're uncomfortable with, it's time to reevaluate the horse. Your safety

LIFE ON THE TRAIL

Buyer Beware!

When we first started buying horses, we found it very interesting when dealing with horse traders (people who buy, sell and trade horses as a business). One particular horse trader sold us a beautiful palomino mare and told us how great she was on the trail. The man knew we were "green." I believe it was written across our foreheads. He sold us the horse for $600 and told us if the horse didn't work out he would buy her back. After several trail rides it was easy to see that I couldn't handle the horse. She was constantly running away with me and I couldn't control her. So, we took the horse back to the horse trader. He immediately started looking over the horse very carefully, pointing out every flaw the horse had. We stood there absolutely dumbfounded. This wonderful horse he'd sold us two weeks earlier had suddenly turned into an old nag with all kinds of deficiencies. Because of the horse's flaws, he said, he would give us $400 for her. Well, we certainly learned a valuable lesson: Buyer beware, especially of traders selling horses.

Dogs are a fact of life on the trail. Do they bother the horse you're trying out?

and that of those around you are the most important considerations.

After you ride him a while and you feel a little more comfortable, take him out on a moderate trail to see how he maneuvers. If this goes well, you might want to try more difficult trails to see how he does. Notice if he trips over everything. That's something you might not be able to change; however, sometimes tripping is a problem your farrier can correct. At this point you might want to take him to a busy trail to see how he reacts to dogs, cars, ATVs and bikes.

After the trial trail rides, decide if the prospect's behavior is something that you can deal with. Be honest with yourself about your abilities to handle the animal. It might be a lot easier to find another horse than to try to correct this one's faults.

More Considerations

It's a good idea to take your own saddle along and see if it fits the horse you're thinking about buying. If it doesn't, are you prepared to buy another that will fit him? You might also want to bring along your husband's/wife's horse for a ride to see how they get along.

Don't be fooled by a horse that "even a child can ride," especially if you're over 50. Older folks and children don't ride the same way, even if you've ridden all your life. Besides, horses seem to know the difference.

We've all heard of people who bought a horse they thought was docile until they got him home. When they rode him for the first

Horses react differently to different situations. Note how the trail prospect handles scary objects.

time out on the trail, he turned into a spitfire. Horses might react differently to strange surroundings, different people, their treatment and many other things. Make sure the horse behaves the way you want him to. If you don't feel safe, sell the horse and find one that will take good care of you. Don't be emotional when buying your horse. When it comes down to what's more important – his looks, his pedigree or his performance – there should be no discussion. His performance should be your first consideration.

When buying a trail horse, it's important to think clearly about your objective, how you're going to be riding the horse and your future goals. Use your head, not your heart.

4 EQUIPMENT

Good, functional equipment is necessary for the comfort and safety of both horse and rider. This horse wears an Australian saddle and a bitless bridle.

As you would in any sport, in trail riding you must have good equipment to enjoy the activity to its fullest. Ill-fitting and faulty equipment is uncomfortable for you and your horse and can even cause serious, potentially life-threatening, problems. Any trail, but especially those in the backcountry, can be challenging enough without having to worry about your comfort and safety, a tired or sore horse or broken tack. The right equipment can help alleviate some of the extra stress on you and your horse.

Good tack can last you a lifetime and it's worth the extra dollars it takes to buy quality equipment. It'll be the cheapest and best thing you can do for yourself, and the safest for you and your horse.

Your Saddle

Your saddle is a critical piece of equipment and needs to be substantial enough to hold up to the type of abuse it'll receive on the trail. Trees limbs, sharp rocks and a number of other things can do serious damage to your equipment, especially your saddle. If your horse happens to roll over on it, it certainly needs to withstand the punishment.

Saddles are like breeds of horses. People have their own ideas and prejudices as to what works. Things like horses, saddles, equipment and even hauling rigs are also influenced by the area of the country you're in, and perhaps the horse group you ride with. Don't let regional fashion be your guide, however. Ride a saddle that's right for you and your horse.

It's my opinion that western and Australian saddles might give the rider a more secure seat on difficult trails, as many are designed with deep seats, high cantles and adequate swells to help keep a person in the saddle. Deep seats are particularly safer than ones you can easily slide out of. A saddle that has a flat seat can let you glide off if your horse jumps unexpectedly, stumbles or just maneuvers through rough country.

That said, I realize there are a lot of English riders, who are more familiar with hunt- and dressage-type saddles, and many of them have deep knee rolls to help stabilize the rider. If this is your saddle of choice, that's fine. Ride whatever makes you comfortable and feel safe.

An absolute must is to make sure your saddle fits your horse properly. If your horse develops a saddle sore or girth gall, he won't be much fun to ride, and maybe you won't be able to ride him at all. A well-fitting saddle sits down on a horse's back. You should be able to see an even sweat pattern when you remove the saddle pads after a ride. The saddle's bars shouldn't bridge over the horse's back, leaving gaps you can see or feel with your hands.

High swells and a high cantle make for a deep seat on this western saddle.

Wide-bottomed stirrups spread out foot pressure. Note, that the boot has a riding heel and is also a good boot to walk in, should the need arise.

Saddles that bridge put an extreme amount of pressure on the horse and even cause him to go mysteriously lame. You might think the lameness is in his feet, when the pain actually originated in his back from a saddle that fits poorly. Your horse will find himself having to compensate in his gait, and, over time, he'll come up sore in his legs and feet.

The saddle shouldn't sit down on or pinch the horse's withers at all. Such pressure causes the horse pain and eventually a saddle sore. Again, the pain can possibly make the horse move differently and he might become lame.

Perhaps you've never had a problem with your saddle on your horse before, but find one after a particularly difficult ride. Riding different terrain is like walking in dress shoes that you've worn for years in town, and then you try hiking in the mountains with them. They probably won't be comfortable because they'll

LIFE ON THE TRAIL

Caught in the Act

As we were riding up a steep hill, one of the ladies in our group leaned forward to get under a tree limb and caught her bra on her saddle horn. This made it a little difficult for her to sit back up in her saddle. In addition to being embarrassed, she also got the giggles, which became contagious. We all stopped to give her a chance to free herself and to give us a chance for a big laugh.

It's not uncommon for people, as they dismount, to catch their clothing on the horn. It's hard to get clothes untangled while dangling from the saddle. And you certainly can't get yourself free without someone in the group noticing.

The cruppers on these saddles will help keep the saddles from sliding forward should this couple encounter steep, downhill terrain.

put pressure on parts of your feet you never used for walking before. Get the point?

On the other hand, if you're hurting, you won't want to ride for very long either.

There could be other reasons why you might become uncomfortable in a saddle you've used for years without any problems. As your rides become longer and tougher, you might find they bring out some issues you haven't had before. Two common problems are knee and ankle pain, which can usually be alleviated with flexible stirrup leathers or stirrups that can swivel, thus taking the pressure off your legs to remain in one position for hours. Riding differently can make a difference in how your body responds. In fact, as we get older, our needs change along with our bodies. Your equipment, especially your saddle, might have to change, too.

Saddle Horn

If you ride in a saddle that has a horn, you might want one as low to the saddle as possible. Saddle horns can be dangerous in rough country. You can get hurt if you fall or lean forward onto a horn. People have broken ribs and much worse when a horse has fallen on them, or the person fell forward and became impaled by the horn. This is especially true for horns that stick up high above the saddle, such as those on roping or cutting horse saddles.

Stirrups and Stirrup Leathers

As mentioned above, it's best to have some flexibility in your stirrup leathers. You'll only have to bang your knee on a tree trunk, scrape your leg on a fence or hit your shin on a boulder once or twice to make you aware of how you need to get your body out of harm's way quickly. One good way of doing this is to have free-moving stirrup leathers. You can bend your leg back, forward or out to the side and never have to take your foot out of the stirrup. Then you can carry on with your ride without fighting to get your foot back into the stirrup. Some western saddle fenders are very wide and rigid. What you're looking for are those that swing back and forth easily. English and Australian stirrup leathers don't have this problem. They're narrow to begin with and are very flexible.

Like other aspects of your tack, stirrups are personal preference. Almost any stirrup will do for light trail riding, but if you intend to go for many miles, lightweight stirrups that are wide provide the best platform for all-day riding.

LIFE ON THE TRAIL

Broken Buckles, Broken Ribs

On one of our rides, my husband Jim turned in his saddle to talk to me and, as he did, he put all his weight into one stirrup. Before I knew what happened, Jim and one of his new stirrups were on the ground. His horse Smoke immediately stopped and looked down at his rider, seemingly as amazed as I was. Thank goodness we weren't too far from our rig so we could walk back, very slowly. Jim's fall and his broken ribs were caused by a defective buckle. The saddle was fairly new, and we hadn't looked at the stirrup leathers closely. This incident taught us a lesson: Don't take anything for granted, not even a new saddle.

They spread out the pressure on your feet and help keep you from becoming sore.

Cinches or Girths

There are many choices in cinches or girths, and most are made from either natural or synthetic materials. Few cinches for western saddles are better than the traditional 100-percent mohair string cinch. The natural fibers wick moisture and have some "give" to them, so they're comfortable against a horse's rib cage and when a horse breathes.

Synthetic cinches, such as those made out of nylon or neoprene or some other man-made material, are popular among the performance-horse crowd because they're easy to wash off. However, they might not be the best choice for long trail rides since there's little to no give

LIFE ON THE TRAIL

Down for the Count

My husband Jim, our teenage son Clint and I were riding in the Flat Top Wilderness of Colorado, and stopped at a stream to allow our horses to drink. While they drank, we enjoyed a conversation about the beautiful area when all of a sudden Clint's horse dropped to the ground with a thud. Luckily Clint landed clear of his horse. We were all startled, but within a few seconds his horse was back up and looking around, seemingly as puzzled as we were. After some investigation, we found that his breast collar had, in all probability, cut off his air while he was bending down to reach the water. From that day on, we checked our horses' breast collars frequently and loosened them when our horses drank.

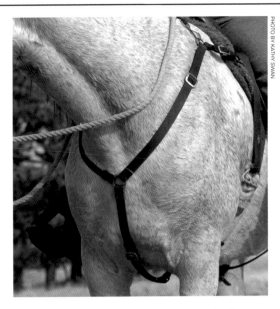

A properly fitted breast collar rests at the base of the neck and is adjusted so that it doesn't interfere with the horse's shoulder movement. Also, note that on this breast collar the connecting strap from the collar ring to the cinch D-ring isn't too tight.

This rider's unique saddle incorporates his horn bags and saddlebags.

LIFE ON THE TRAIL

Don't Bet Your Life on It

In my saddlebag, in addition to all of the essentials, I carry a gift from our friend Larry Bailey, a magnesium bar in a leather case with a striker and some very fine wood sticks that I can use to start a fire. I also have a small can with some emergency gear that could save my life. (Well, that's what it says on the can.) It contains some matches (just in case my magnesium bar and striker don't work), a stick of chewing gum, string, a fishhook and other similar objects. I hope I'll never have to open it up and bet my life on these things.

in them. They should work just fine, though, for short-distance rides.

Leather girths, like the kind used on English and Australian saddles, are good trail choices. Their "hide-against-hide" feature makes them comfortable for horses and many have flexible straps for their buckle adjustments, providing even more give than a mohair string cinch.

Collars and Cruppers

A breast collar and a crupper (or crouper) are two pieces of equipment that can be very handy, especially if you're riding in hilly or mountainous areas. They help stabilize a saddle and keep it from sliding forward or back when you tackle steep terrain. You want to be prepared for whatever you'll find along the way. You're better off having a breast collar and a crupper on your horse and not needing them than being caught on a trail where you need them and don't have them. You also won't have to stop numerous times to adjust your saddle because it shifted.

Neither piece of equipment should be too tight nor too loose. The center ring on the breast collar should lie comfortably at the base of the horse's neck. Always hook up the connecting strap that goes from the collar's center ring to the D-ring on the cinch, and make sure it doesn't bind the horse. The horse's shoulders should be able to move freely so take care that the collar isn't tight.

Adjust the crupper to have some play in it, as well. You don't want it constantly grabbing the horse around his tail, possibly rubbing him, but you don't want it flopping all over the place either.

It's always a good idea to introduce any equipment to your horse at home before you hit the trail. Do so slowly, especially with the crupper. Having something around his tail can really bother a horse, so let him get used to it long before you ride him with it.

Tie-downs

Tie-downs are straps that connect the bridle to the breast collar or cinch as a means of controlling a high-headed horse. It prevents the horse from rooting his nose and evading the bit. They're generally not thought of as trail equipment, although some riders feel they need them for an extra measure of control.

If you use one on your horse, unfasten it when crossing deep water. If a horse needs to swim, the tie-down might make it impossible for him to get his head up out of the water. Horses with tie-downs on have been known to drown while crossing water.

Saddlebags

What you take along with you on your ride can mean the difference between having a great day or a bad one.

Everyone has his or her own idea as to what's important. Access to some items is so important that I carry them in a pocket or on a belt clip.

With a good pair of saddlebags or a cantle bag, along with a horn bag you can carry most of the things you might need for comfort and safety. Some important items include equine and human first-aid kits, a pair of binoculars, hoof pick, bug spray, and an Easyboot® or some emergency hoof boot. Other items you might sometimes want to carry are a saw, a gun (and permit if required), pepper spray, a mileage meter and your lunch.

Horn bags are great for things you need easy access to, such as a water bottle, sunscreen, chap-stick, gloves, Kleenex, camera, global positioning system (GPS), compass, cell phone or snacks. Reminder: Your GPS might not operate in mountainous terrain, canyon country or dense forests.

Strings

There are a few things that might be handy to have, but don't have to be stored away. Leather strings on rings are useful for tying things, such as jackets and rain gear, to your saddle. They can also be used out on the trail to repair faulty equipment. Snaps or clips can also attach things to the rings.

Your belt is a good place to wear things you might need quick access to and things you wouldn't want to be without if you become separated from your horse. This might include such things as a pocketknife or multi-tool and pepper spray.

Saddle pads

Saddle pads come in a variety of materials, shapes and sizes. Modern materials have made saddle pads much more effective and comfortable for your horse. Some pads can keep the pressure even on your horse's back, thus alleviating dry spots caused by undue pressure. Others are especially good at not slipping under your saddle.

One good pad and maybe a Navajo-type blanket are all that should be necessary. Too

You can carry lots of stuff on a saddle with lots of strings.

many thick pads under your saddle cause you to have to cinch up too tightly, and they can make you feel top heavy in the saddle. Also, too many pads don't allow you to hang your legs down naturally for close contact with your horse's sides.

If your saddle fits your horse well, the pad will help offer extra protection, but it can't solve all the problems of an ill-fitting saddle.

Bits and Spurs

There have been many books written on the subject of bits and spurs, and this book doesn't address the art and science of these tools.

LIFE ON THE TRAIL

Not a Bit

At an organized trail ride in Tennessee, a man rode up beside me and asked what I was using to control my horse. I tried to say that it was a jaquima (Spanish for hackamore or bitless bridle), but before I could get the words out, he replied "You can't control that horse without a bit in his mouth." I looked at the stranger a little puzzled and replied that I was doing very well with my apparatus and that my horse had never run away with me. I explained that I'd had several other horses that had run off while wearing a bit. He had to eat his words and leave.

Obviously, however, you need knowledge and experience to use them correctly.

When it comes to bits, the main thing is selecting one that fits your horse. It should be wide enough for your horse's mouth and

LIFE ON THE TRAIL

Up and Over

A group of riders had congregated in an open area for a break. In the middle of the crowd stood a man, who had decided for whatever reason, not to tie his horse to a tree like everyone else. While talking, the man dropped a rein, the horse stepped on it and when he jerked back, he reared up and continued over on his back. The crowd was quick enough to scatter, and no one was hit by the falling horse.

The rider makes sure the bridle is adjusted for a comfortable fit.

Short, dull rowels are all that should be necessary in the way of trail spurs. Note the good riding heel on the boot.

adjusted so that it creates no wrinkles in his lips. Years ago, there was a theory that the bridle should be adjusted to create one or two wrinkles, but that's an old wives' tale. Prying the horse's lips back for hours is cruel.

Many horses handle well in bitless bridles or hackamores (called "jaquima" in Spanish), or even in halters, and never need a metal bit in their mouths. True hackamores work off nose pressure alone. There are also mechanical hackamores, which consist of shanks to which the reins are attached and a curb strap. They work off curb action, like a curb bit, but they rely solely on leverage under the horse's jaw and don't involve the mouth.

If your horse is well broke enough to ride without a bit, by all means, do so. Having no metal in his mouth is far more comfortable for him, especially on long rides, than packing steel.

Unfortunately, over the years, I've seen many accidents involving bits, most of them having to do with poor horsemanship and not the equipment itself. It can be a serious problem when a horse steps on a dropped rein or pulls back when the reins are tied to a tree.

As for spurs, some horses need them and some don't. Typically, however, spurs with short, dull rowels are all you should need on a good trail horse. Kicking a horse accidentally with a spur has caused many an accident out on the trail.

Shoes and Other Protective Footwear

Your horse's feet are something you need to attend to and be aware of at all times. If your horse comes up lame, you have no horse. You simply can't ride a crippled horse.

It's best to have your horse shod on a regular basis and, if possible, just before you go on a trip. That way your horse can become comfortable in his new shoes, and you can detect any problems ahead of time.

Adding a traction material to your horse's shoes is a common practice in some parts of the country. Two of the most common additives are borium-tipped nails or borium welded onto the shoe itself. With borium-tipped nails, the usual practice is to replace four of the nails in each shoe and use regular horseshoe nails in the rest of the shoe.

Having borium welded onto the shoe itself is very controversial. It has long been known that this traction substance used on a gaited horse's shoes can interfere with the animal's gait. When a shoe with borium hits a hard surface, it doesn't

A good hat, gloves and sunglasses protect a rider from the elements.

allow the foot to slide, which interferes with the natural breakover action of the horse's hoof. It can cause leg and hoof problems if used over a long period of time. If you're going to use this product, please use it with care.

If you prefer not to use a traction material on your horse's shoes, but feel that you need some traction for your horse, you may want to talk to your farrier about other shoe considerations. For example, rim shoes have been shown to work well on slick surfaces.

Since horses carry most of their weight on their front feet, some trail riders have their horses shod on the front only. However, rocky areas can be hard on any horse's hoofs. The only way you can find out if your horse can withstand the rocks is ride him in them. If his feet hold up, then leave him barefoot behind.

Riding the horse barefoot, front and back, is always an option, and is a trend among many horsemen. There are horses whose hoofs are good enough to tolerate going barefoot, but you'll need to talk to a specialist in this form of trimming. It's not wise to make the decision without talking to a natural-hoof-care professional.

One increasingly popular hoof-protection choice is hoof boots. There are dozens of

Chaps come in mighty handy while riding in "prickly" country. Notice that this pair has a useful pouch for stuffing essentials.

different kinds on the market and more being invented all the time. Hoof boots are intended for use on barefoot horses or for emergencies if you lose a shoe. Put them on only when you ride your horse; otherwise keep him in his natural state. That's better for your horse anyway.

Another alternative is applying hoof hardener or a protective coating over the sole and outer rim of the wall, not the frog. These substances allow the horse to use his natural hoof mechanism (expansion and contraction upon movement), something steel shoes don't permit.

Protective Garments

Chaps, chinks or half chaps are very useful, especially when riding across rough country. In addition to keeping your riding pants a little cleaner, leggings sure help protect you from the weather, and, if they're waterproof, they keep you dry in the rain or snow.

Another protective garment you can't go riding without is a pair of gloves. They protect your hands from "rein burn," the weather, sunburn and all those nasty branches and trees that can get in your way.

Cowboy hats have long been a staple for the trail rider. Cowboys wear them for a good reason: The wearer is protected from the sun, wind, rain and overhanging tree limbs. The larger the brim, the better for protection against sunburn. Also, safety-certified riding helmets are becoming more popular all across the country, as riders are becoming more safety-conscious.

A good pair of boots can save your feet and toes from suffering major damage if your horse takes a wrong step – on you! However, their main reason is to help keep your feet in the stirrups, and, thus, you in the saddle. All good riding boots have heels tall enough to

LIFE ON THE TRAIL

These Boots Are Made for Walking

One time when I was riding in the Smoky Mountains, my horse lost a shoe, and I found myself walking out on a very steep and rough trail back to camp. The cowboy boots I was wearing sure looked good, but their beauty didn't prevent all the blisters I suffered. I never wore them again while trail riding. I wear boots that I can walk in.

stop your boots from sliding all the way through the stirrups, thus preventing a hang-up should you fall from your horse.

Your footwear should be supportive enough that you're comfortable with your feet in the stirrups all day. Last, but certainly not least, your boots should be comfortable enough to walk in should your trail ride turn into a hike. You never know when you might have to walk back to camp.

Modern riding equipment has become safer, but nothing is foolproof in every situation. Don't expect anything to be 100-percent reliable and, therefore, cast caution to the wind. There'll always be a way for a horse, or circumstances, to undo even the best equipment. Nothing ruins a ride faster than tack that makes you or your horse uncomfortable or breaks at just the wrong moment.

LIFE ON THE TRAIL

Don't "Bor-ium" Me

My experience with borium welded on my horse's shoes hasn't been a good one. It interfered with Max's gait and made him stumble. In fact, after the second set of borium shoes, Max became extremely unsafe to ride. I wasn't sure what was going on until it was too late. One day, while we were riding down a rocky trail, Max stumbled and fell down. Unfortunately, we were on the edge of a small embankment, which made him fall onto his side, trapping me. As I recovered from my broken ankle, I had a long time to reflect on the situation. On three occasions, Max had fallen down completely while he had borium on his shoes. He'd not fallen down before the borium shoes, nor after they were taken off. I can't be sure that borium was the culprit, but it seemed that way. Even so, I'm not saying that borium on shoes causes horses to fall down. Shoeing horses, like everything else, is an individual matter and must be considered on a case-by-case basis.

5 ADVICE FOR THE NOVICE RIDER

When you're "out there," sometimes trust in your horse and your friends is all you have to count on.

Before I delve too deeply into the world of the trail rider, I need to address the concerns of novice riders. You might be just beginning your horseback riding career or possibly getting back into horses after a long absence. Marriage, kids, college, work, you name it. Lots of things keep us from our horses. Whatever your situation, now that you've decided to take the plunge, you might be dealing with some issues that you'll need to resolve in order to enjoy the sport to its fullest. Unlike arena riding, where you're safely encircled by a fence, trail riding in the outdoors is wide open, and along with that can come some fear of riding and the unknown. After all, you're staking your life on the back of a 1,000-pound animal whose main survival instinct is to flee from danger. That could translate into some scary moments. Here's some advice to help you deal with your fears.

Where Does It Come From

Fear can come from anywhere and for a variety of reasons. Accidents and getting hurt are the most obvious reasons. However, there are times when fear can creep into your trail riding simply because of the situation you find yourself in. How would you know you're afraid of trails that follow the edge of a cliff, especially if you've never ridden these kinds of trails before? There are times when unforeseen events can bring the element of fear right out of the blue.

If you have the right mindset you can develop a way of dealing with these unexpected circumstances. We all know that what we think affects the way we feel. Positive thinking and attitude are so important in overcoming any negativity in your riding experience. Remember that fear is only a temporary feeling. You can triumph over it with experience, time and a willing attitude.

As you progress through your new trail riding life, don't concentrate on your bouts with fear; shake them off as fast as you can. Instead focus your energies on the adrenalin rush you get when you accomplish a new feat, the feeling of achievement when you reach your trail riding goals, such as your first ride across a wide stream. Before long your negative feelings will be fewer and you can begin enjoying every ride.

Fear has a way of interfering with your riding abilities. It can throw you off balance. Unfortunately, when you're afraid, all your weight seems to be in the upper part of your body. You feel like you're teetering around on top of your horse, sort of a Humpty Dumpty, just waiting to fall. Any time you get off balance, even a little, your chances of falling off your horse increase. The more off balance you

LIFE ON THE TRAIL

Never to Return

Once, in the wilderness of Montana, we were on a trail that seemed to slough off, right underneath my horse's feet. In fact, as I followed the horse in front of me, I could see the earth and rocks crash down the hillside. I kept telling myself to be calm and just get to solid footing. As we reached the other side of the hill, I was relieved to know we were on a loop trail and we didn't have to come back the same way. However, we soon discovered that the trail ended at a rockslide and we couldn't continue any farther. I couldn't believe we'd have to return to camp on that terrible trail. However, when we reached the hillside, I led my horse across to the other side and had a safe trip back to camp.

get, the more afraid, and then the more unbalanced and the cycle continues. Talk about feeding your fear.

I've experienced my share of fears over the years. As an older beginner rider, I had to overcome my fear of a terrible fall early in my riding experience. My first accident, in which I sustained numerous injuries including several broken bones, left me with a debilitating fear I wasn't sure that I could, or wanted, to overcome. The recurring challenges made my trail riding experience different than that of most riders, but they've also made my journey a tremendous learning experience and literally a life-changing event.

Nowadays, it's hard for me to believe how I felt back in the days, months and years after my accident. When I go back to the places where I first started riding and remember the fear that I had then, I'm proud of myself and how far I've come. Knowing my husband Jim and I did whatever it took to get me over my fear has done nothing but make me a much better rider.

You do have to figure on dealing with accidents and setbacks. Even the best of riders will have a fall once in awhile. But, the more positive you feel about your experiences, the better you can deal with the negatives.

The Right Horse

One good way to ward off fear is to have the right horse. A horse you can trust is a

LIFE ON THE TRAIL

Have No Fear, Max is Here

In my early riding career, my stiff, fearful riding position caused me quite a few problems while I was trying to learn to relax. One time, my horse jumped when I wasn't expecting it. He catapulted me right over his head, and I landed on the ground in front of him. Of course, I was on a ride with a few hundred people at the time.

Another time he jumped a log, I fell forward on to his neck, slid down and underneath him. What a scary event. All I could see was his belly and all four feet jumping around trying to stay off of me. Thank goodness for a great horse.

priceless animal, and one that will help give you peace of mind. As you know, there are no guarantees with horses. This sport has its own inherent dangers. In fact, you'll be hard-pressed to find anyone in the horse community who hasn't had his/her share of accidents with their equine friends.

Picking a trustworthy horse isn't always that easy. It might be to your advantage to have an older horse, 7 years or older, that has lots of trail experience. The older horse can do a lot for your self-confidence and feeling of safety.

Another way to help overcome some of your insecurities is to learn all you can about your horse by spending as much time with him as you can. Take over his feeding, if someone else does that for you, and groom him daily. Longeing or round-penning is another great way to make a connection with your horse. The idea is to have as much interaction as possible.

The Right Equipment

Choosing the right equipment to go along with your experienced horse can also help you feel safer. Pick a comfortable saddle that feels like it'll keep you in it and on your mount. (See Chapter 4 titled "Equipment.")

For serious protection, you can wear an ASTM-certified helmet, and there are also riding vests that help safeguard your vital organs. Don't be embarrassed to use protective gear. It's important to keep your mind on your riding and the safer you are, the better you'll feel, which in turn helps your confidence. And, in case there's an accident, your injuries will probably be less severe and you'll

recover more quickly. These things are your insurance policy for a safer and better ride. Go for it!

Experience is the Best Teacher

Riding your horse is the best way to overcome some of your fears; experience is the best teacher and one of the best ways to ward off your anxiety. Each time you ride, even for a short time, you gain a little confidence. The more you ride and the more positive experiences you have, the better you feel. Start slow and for a short time, increasing your time on the horse as you progress. The important thing is to ride, ride, ride.

However, you'll find riding to be much more pleasurable when you ride on trails where you feel safe, especially if you're a beginning rider. Familiar trails give you the security of knowing what to expect and what's in store for you. Also, going slow and taking your time help a lot.

Max has proven over and over again that he's the right horse for Janine.

Riding helmets are popular pieces of safety equipment.

When you find yourself in a spot that gives you the willies, get off your horse and walk. You might choose to lead him through the tough area or you can let someone pony him while you walk. Do whatever makes you feel comfortable.

Riding Buddies

You'll find the most helpful people involved in your quest to overcome your fear are the horsemen you ride with. People who care about you and respect your fear can help you conquer it. Knowing these folks support what you're doing and won't give you a hard time because you're afraid can make a big difference. It's frightening to think the people you're riding with might just ride off and leave you behind. Attitude and caring from fellow riders can make a big difference and boost your fragile outlook.

Spousal Support

Husbands sometimes wonder why their wives won't go riding with them. Perhaps if husbands became more cognizant of their wives' fears and acted accordingly, more wives would give it a try. Actually, the roles can also be reversed, with beginning-rider husbands being the ones needing confidence from their "horse-crazy" wives. Be attentive to

Whenever a tricky area concerns you, don't be ashamed to get off and lead your horse, if that makes you feel more safe and secure.

Having experienced riding partners is the best way for a novice to begin trail riding.

your partner's needs while out on the trail. Keep a close eye out for your spouse and show you're there for him or her. Believe me, you'll have a very grateful riding partner. As your or your partner's confidence grows, so will your riding outings. Soon you two will be riding all the time.

This might sound like a "no brainer" to some of us but it's an all-too-common occurrence with couples. Let's just say it's generally a result of a lack of communication and not a total disregard for the partner. Most people don't want to admit they're afraid and, therefore, just don't think to talk it over with their loved ones. Unfortunately, some people give up riding rather than deal with the problem. Don't let that be your situation.

6 THE TRAIL HORSE'S SKILLS

Savvy trail horses sense what lies ahead.

Horses have survived in the wild for millions of years, long before man domesticated them. This gives them a rather long history of maneuvering and functioning successfully in the great outdoors. Horses have instincts that we as humans don't fully understand, but what's lucky for us as trail riders is that they all come into play in a good trail horse.

An experienced horse that's in tune with his environment makes your enjoyment of the ride all that much greater. For instance, a savvy trail horse can show you where the trail is, especially when it seems to disappear.

He can determine whether you should enter a questionable area, such as hidden quicksand or a bog. He can keep you informed of your surroundings by letting you know if there's a wild animal nearby or someone's approaching you. He can even keep you from getting lost.

Here are some of the instincts and abilities of a trail-savvy horse.

Trail Blazer

You'll be amazed at how your horse knows exactly where the trail is. This, of course, is most apparent when he's never been on a particular trail before. Horses simply have an uncanny ability to know where to find the trail. This is true for trails hidden under fallen leaves or in thick weeds, fresh fallen snow or old trails that have faded over years of non-use. Some horses can find their trail over a solid rock surface where they traveled earlier in the day. Whether this is a natural ability or something they've been able to develop over the years, the fact is the more miles of trails they cover the better they become at this skill.

Not realizing that a horse has this ability, a rider oftentimes ignores his horse when the animal tries to follow his trail-wise instincts. Over time, the horse gives in to his rider's desires and lets the rider's decision override his own. It's often the wrong choice. Sometimes a horse's biggest obstacle is his human rider.

Memories Are Made of This

Horses have incredible memories. It's not uncommon for them to remember places or things years later. They could literally have ridden thousands of miles and hundreds of different trails in the interim. Upon their return to an area, they're likely to stop at the same spot used as a lunch break before, or take a trail that they'd taken years ago, especially if that trail heads back to the trailer.

This tremendous asset also has a negative side. Your horse will remember unpleasant experiences as well as good ones. If he once perceived something or some place as dangerous, he'll likely never forget it. His apprehension might make no sense to you, but it makes perfect sense to him. For example, your horse might have an inordinate fear of mailboxes or real estate signs. You know they're perfectly harmless, but he thinks of them as horse-

LIFE ON THE TRAIL

Where's the Trailer?

Our horses always seem to know what direction they're going in. If we happen to be going in the wrong direction, in their eyes, then they try to travel at a much slower pace than if they're headed back to the trailer.

A little game I play with my horse while out on the trail is "Where's the trailer?" Sometimes, when I lose my sense of direction, an easy way for me to get myself orientated again is to give my horse his head. Without fail, he'll pick up speed and turn in the direction of the trailer, which gives me my bearings. Then we turn back to the direction I originally was going and my horse goes back to his "non-back to the trailer speed."

eating monsters. It's possible that, somewhere in the past, the wind accidentally opened the mailbox or blew down the sign just when your horse passed it. To him, the monster jumped out to get him. When this sort of incident happens, work through it with your horse as quietly and confidently as you can. Hopefully, someday his faith in you will override his fear.

Another interesting thing about a horse's memory or intellect is the way his brain

An experienced trail horse can pick out the trail, even over rocky terrain.

LIFE ON THE TRAIL

The Nose Knows

Jim and I were riding along on a mesa in Utah's canyon country, filling our eyes with all the beauty below us, when suddenly Max came to an abrupt halt. I could see out of the corner of my eye that Smoke did the same thing. Then Max took small slow steps backward and I could see his nostrils flare as he took in large breaths. I turned to see Smoke doing the same. I looked forward again and began to closely scope out the area in front of me for any movement in the trees and rocks. I rubbed Max's neck and talked calmly to him. I tried to move him to the left, hoping to go away from whatever was out there. However, Max didn't want to go.

We waited a minute or so, then Max moved forward very slowly and deliberately as he began smelling the ground. He continued surveying the area with his nose as Smoke and Dee, our Golden Retriever, came up beside him and began doing the same. What a sight! After a thorough investigation the three seemed to be satisfied with what they had found and let us move on. However, while they were sniffing, I once again glanced around the area. Then I spotted a cougar slinking behind some huge boulders and out of sight. Perhaps that cat had been in that very spot earlier in the day. A cougar's scent would certainly get our horses' attention.

He'll become extremely focused and agitated, even if the threat isn't in sight. You'll see his reaction intensify. He'll also probably snort as he tries to catch the animal's scent.

This kind of reaction on the part of your horse warrants your utmost attention. You can either wait it out, hoping the threat goes away, or you can find another way to travel around it. However, do take his reaction seriously.

Up- and Downhill

The next time you're in the great outdoors, take a look at the paths of wild animals or livestock trails. They usually don't go straight up or down a hill. The path is almost always at an angle. Going straight up or down a steep grade is very hard on a horse. It stresses him excessively and tires him more quickly, leaving him vulnerable to an accident or injury.

When negotiating a steep hill, especially one without a trail, give your horse his head and he'll naturally choose to move at an angle, or he might zigzag his way to get safely to the bottom. His pattern usually depends on the steepness of the hillside. Angling his body allows the horse to keep his 1,000-pound body mass under control. So, allow your horse to pick his way.

LIFE ON THE TRAIL

On Point

One time while riding in Colorado's Flat Top Wilderness with a few of our favorite riding buddies, we'd stopped to have lunch in an aspen grove. Some of us had turned our horses loose in the nearby meadow so they'd have the opportunity to feast on the wonderful mountain grass. One of our friends suddenly remarked, "Hey, look at Smoke; boy, he looks like a bird dog. I've never seen a horse point before." We all took a look at Smoke.

Then we heard another friend say, "Over there, it's a mountain lion." We saw an animal moving across a meadow about a half mile away. The animal was too far away to really tell. One of our friends got out his trusty binoculars and took away all suspense by verifying that the cougar was indeed just a coyote. It would've made for a much better story if we'd seen an elusive mountain lion. However, we wouldn't have seen either if it hadn't been for our "pointing" Smoke.

processes things. His association-skills aren't the same as ours. A horse acts differently when he's running free than when he's being led or when he has a rider on his back. This is true if you're trying to simulate the trail in your back yard, then take your horse out on the trail and expect the same result. He might not act the same way. If one thing is out of place or in the wrong place, he doesn't relate to it in the same way. For example, a horse can live in the same pasture with a herd of cows and even boss them around. Take him out of the pasture, put a saddle on him and ride him down the trail and his reaction to a cow might be totally different. He might act as if he's never seen one before.

Wild About Animals

Your horse has the ability to tell you when there are other animals around. He'll also let you know if he thinks the animal is dangerous or not. For example, when he spots or senses a deer, he'll look at it and move his ears in its direction. After he determines it's okay, he'll continue on his way, unbothered by the intrusion.

On the other hand, if your horse senses the animal is a real danger to him, he'll usually stop and refuse to move toward the threat.

The most natural way for a horse to travel on a steep hillside is at an angle.

Crossing Water

Horses, if given the chance, have a safe and effective way of getting through water. However, many riders, after entering a stream or river, keep their horses going until they reach the other side. If a horse tries to lower his head, thinking he wants to drink, the rider pulls his head up and urges him on. This isn't the way a horse wants to cross.

Instead, give your horse time to take a drink, if he wants one. Then, give him the chance to look things over. Remember, the footing can be tricky, ranging from deep mud or sand to small rocks or big boulders. There might even be some hidden quicksand.

Whether water is shallow or deep, clear or murky, your horse might stop periodically and put his head down, sometimes touching his muzzle to the water. He's actually checking things out the same way he makes his way through any trail. Give him the opportunity to use his natural instincts and senses to cross the trail, especially if it's in the water.

But don't let him "play" in the water, i.e. stand still and splash with a front foot. This can be a prelude to an unexpected dunking for the rider. When crossing a fairly wide body of water (a lazy stream, as opposed to a swift, narrow creek), or pausing to water your horse at the edge of a pond or lake, watch out that he doesn't suddenly decide to lie down. A sweaty horse who encounters a cool body of water on a hot day often finds the temptation to lie down in the water just too good to pass up. Here's a common scenario.

The horse pauses to drink and then seems to relax, just like the rider, enjoying the moment. If he's on the edge of a pond or lake, he'll casually take another step or two into deeper water. Turn him back toward shore immediately. If you don't react quickly, this is the moment he'll unexpectedly fold or drop his front legs underneath him in an effort to lie down and roll – with you on him – just to cool off. A horse who dunks his rider can make for a great joke, afterwards – as long as no one drowned.

Note: One way to tell if a horse is drinking is to look at his throat. If he's not swallowing, he's not drinking. I know that sounds like a no-brainer, but have you ever checked? We all assume that if a horse's head is down to the water the horse is drinking.

Detective Work

An experienced trail horse has the ability to let you know when it's unsafe to enter an area.

Allow your horse to investigate the water before venturing in.

It's common for horses to sniff the water and look carefully as they cross.

LIFE ON THE TRAIL

Equine Water Bottle

One such astonishing thing our horses do on the trail is save water for later. When we come upon a source of water, whether it's a stream, pond, puddle or whatever, they'll take a drink as usual. Then down the trail, at some point perhaps hours later, we'll hear them swish the water around in their mouths, and then they swallow it. They actually carry water in their mouths to drink at a later time.

LIFE ON THE TRAIL

Discretion is the Better Part of Valor

While riding in the beautiful Great Smoky Mountains of North Carolina/Tennessee, we happened upon a very boggy area in the trail. It lay between two hills and an old wood walkway to one side. As I stopped to consider whether we should continue on the path with its missing slats or to take our chances in the bog, Max suddenly hunkered down, then leaped the total length of the wooden path and landed on the other side. He used his own discretion and decided that neither was safe, so he avoided them both. I guess he decided to take matters into his own hands, or should I say feet?

This is especially true in boggy areas, muddy places and in quicksand. You can help your horse hone this skill by allowing him to investigate a trail obstacle thoroughly, all the while cultivating his senses. Giving him the time to look closely, to smell the area and to even test the ground by taking a step or two allows your horse to detect any dangers.

Your horse has his own way of doing things. However, if you've taught him to perform his trail tasks in a particular way, there'll be a time when his training will override his natural abilities. At that stage, he might not be able to regain the abilities that were never given the opportunity to

Horses can tell a lot about the trail by smelling it.

develop. Therefore, don't expect all horses to maneuver the trail naturally. Also, there are always exceptions. Not all horses are created equal and, therefore, not all acquire high level trail skills.

A key to success is to recognize that your horse has something to offer your trail riding adventures. If you learn to balance your horse's natural talents and your experience, you'll have a great trail partnership.

Let's Talk

All of your horse's natural instincts and abilities are lost if you don't know how to pay attention to them. Horses are always communicating with us. Unfortunately, most of what a horse tries to say often falls on deaf ears – the human's. It isn't that the rider isn't interested in what the horse has to say. It's just that he or she hasn't taken the time to listen. When riding, you normally divert your attention to your friends or to the trail itself, especially when you have to negotiate tricky obstacles. That doesn't leave much time for watching your horse.

As horsemen, we've been taught through other disciplines that we're in charge and shouldn't let our horses do the thinking. Therefore, knowing when to give your horse his head isn't always a cut-and-dried situation. It's generally something we learn over a long period of time and involves a lot of trial and error. There are times when you'll wonder who's the student, you or your horse. The truth of the matter, you both are.

One of the best ways to learn how your horse communicates is through observation. Watch your horse and take your cues from him. You'll be amazed how this works. Here's some of the more common "sign language."

Ear Language :

Your horse's ears are a good indicator of what's going on around you. Watch his ear movement. It's usually very active. His ears continually move front to back, back to front and side to side. If they stop moving and seem to be in a "holding pattern," take a look in that direction. You might not be able to see what's caught your horse's attention, but without a doubt there's something out there.

When you're riding with a friend, watch your two horses as they work in tandem. The horse in the lead always rotates his ears from the side to the front, taking in his surroundings and noticing what's up ahead on the trail.

Circling a distracted horse helps get his mind back on the trail.

Sensing something in the distance, a horse pricks up his ears.

The horse behind does his job by rotating his ears to take in the areas from his sides to the rear. It's a lot of fun to watch.

Body Language:

Horses express themselves through their bodies. Tense muscles and hyperactivity are signs something is going on with your horse. He's anxious and possibly afraid of something. Horses don't know how to lie, so take a moment to assess the situation and see if you can't resolve his fears.

Your horse can also feel what's going on with you. If you're nervous or afraid, he'll know. This kind of communication is a two-way street. When your horse is nervous, perhaps you should evaluate yourself. Take a moment to calm down. This might be all your horse needs to relax.

Snorting and extending his neck down and outward are also signs of your horse's independence and excitement. This occurs most often when returning on the same trail you went out on. The horse knows he's going back to camp. He's letting you know he's definitely ready to

take matters into his own hands. The proper way to handle this outburst is to take control of the situation and let him know it's time to calm down and get back to the task at hand. This can be done by circling or checking the reins to help put his thoughts back to the trail ride.

As your rapport with your horse grows, you'll learn his body language. You'll know the "feel" of your horse while you're in the saddle. You'll be able to tell when he's anxious and tense and, conversely, when he's relaxed. This'll help you decide when to trust his assessment of a situation. Remember, allowing the horse to make a decision doesn't mean becoming a passenger who's just along for the ride. You're still in charge.

Over the years I've learned to feel my horse through the saddle. I can feel him tense up or relax. I can feel when he's getting ready to act silly or if something upsets him. It's nice to have advance notice to his upcoming behavior. I can usually "cut him off at the pass" before the situation gets out of hand.

The next time you're out on the trail be aware of your horse's body language and attempt to figure out what he's trying to tell you. It's fun and you'll both benefit.

As you become more aware of and understand your horse's instincts and abilities, trail riding will take on a whole new dimension. It becomes a true partnership where you and your horse form a strong bond built on trust, confidence and communication.

7 COMMON TRAIL OBSTACLES

Rock ledges can be tricky obstacles to negotiate.

No matter where you ride, there are always obstacles you and your horse will encounter as you go down the trail. You can try to recreate some in your back yard for training purposes, such as logs to walk over, wood bridges to cross or mud holes to wade through, but nothing can truly simulate the trail. The best and only way to train your trail horse is on the trail, with natural, not man-made obstacles. How you approach an obstacle will leave a lasting impression on your horse, so give him all good experiences and he'll carry you through anything.

It's important to take your time as you maneuver through obstacles and give your horse encouragement. It might help to talk to him in a quiet voice, reassuring him with a "Good boy," or "Easy." Saying anything at all in a calming tone certainly helps. It's best to keep it short and repeat the word over and over as you rub or lightly pat his neck just above the wither area. This helps instill the right attitude for both of you.

You'll undoubtedly encounter obstacles that might create a little doubt or fear in you. Just proceed slowly and deliberately, and, most importantly, learn to relax. Remember, your response to what you're about to do is transmitted to your horse. If you're nervous and excited, your horse will be, as well. If you find your horse becoming upset about his task, take a look at your own reaction. Are you anxious and sitting stiffly in the saddle? If you're relaxed and calm, your horse will, in all likelihood, quiet down also.

In this chapter, I'll cover common trail obstacles and suggest time-tested techniques for tackling them. Plus, I'll also offer pointers in "trail sense." That's the common sense all trail riders need to be safe and enjoy their experiences.

Trail Speed

At the beginning of any ride, walk your horse for the first mile or so. This gives him time to warm up his muscles. It also helps to set the tone for the day's ride.

The best and safest speed to maneuver obstacles on the trail is at a slow pace. A horse can lose his footing if he travels too fast over rocky areas, exposed tree roots, up or down steep hills and through water deeper than a few inches.

Gaiting or trotting your horse is safer in areas where you're familiar with the terrain and footing, and you've a clear view of the trail ahead. Of course, you'll want to keep your speed down, even on flat terrain, at the higher elevations until you and your horse are acclimated.

Open and Shut

Your horse doesn't necessarily have to be able to side-pass in order to open and shut a gate, but it's a handy maneuver to have. Practice at home on an arena or corral gate, so your horse is familiar with moving his body laterally as you open and shut the gate. In side-passing, your horse should move away

The safest trail speed in questionable areas is slow. Savvy horses investigate the ground they walk on, so allow your horse to look and smell it if he chooses.

With a cattle guard on one side and barbed wire and cactus on the other, the rider is careful in opening the gate.

from leg pressure. For instance, in opening a gate with your right hand, press your right leg on your horse's rib cage to move the horse away from the gate as you bring it toward you. When the opening is wide enough to pass safely, maneuver your horse through it and close the gate, this time pressing with your left leg to move your horse to the right.

You might encounter gates that are opened vertically instead of the traditional side-opening gates. These metal farm gates are "counter balanced" at one end; therefore, when you release the latch, the gate moves upward. As in opening the gate in the previous paragraph, you can side-pass to the latch on the gate. However, when you release the latch the gate will move straight up, of its own accord, on the side with the latch. When the gate is high enough, you can proceed through the opening, which will look like an inverted V. When you're on the other

A horse who'll pony quietly alongside another is a big asset at times.

Rocky areas are always tough on horses feet and balance, so slow down.

side of the gate, again side-pass over to the latch. While you're positioned near the latch area, reach up and take hold of the rope or string attached to the gate and give a little tug to start the downward motion of the gate. At that point you can move out of the way. The gate will slowly move back into position and the latch should be self-closing. Gates that swing both ways can be opened and closed easily.

Barbed-wire gates are very common, and you can't safely open them from horseback, so it must be done afoot. There are several approaches to opening gates on foot, and the safest way is to use both hands. If you're riding in company, dismount and give your horse to a friend. Have that person pony (lead) your horse through the opening for you. Of course, your horse should be used to being ponied and not crowd the horse and rider leading him. Otherwise, the two horses could try to get through the gate at the same time and cause a big wreck, injuring all parties.

If you're not confident in how your horse ponies, have your friend hold your horse as you open the gate wide. Then hold your horse as your friend rides through. When the other rider is safely through the gate, walk your horse through and give the reins back to your friend. Then, you can close the gate.

If you're riding alone, look for stout trees nearby and tie your horse while you open and close the gate. If there's nothing to tie to, and that's often the case, hobble your horse (if he knows how) or put on his halter and lead rope and hold your horse at a safe distance as you work with the gate.

On the Rocks

Going slow is the name of the game in negotiating rocky terrain. You don't want your horse blundering through a bunch of rocks. He could lose a shoe or even hurt himself. Allow him to pick his way through the rocks. Between the two of you, he has the best sense of where to put his feet, so give him his head.

However, that doesn't mean you give him a "blank check" either. Watch him very carefully and, if he seems to get off track or starts to be inattentive to his task, then take over the directions. Be careful you don't knock him off balance when taking back control. Don't shift your weight or jerk on the reins. Stay calm and relaxed while guiding him through the area.

An overhanging branch could spell disaster if you're not paying attention.

LIFE ON THE TRAIL

Trail Sweeper

I let the bigger horses go first through the woods. They'll break off any branches and vines, and that makes it easy for me to get through. Also, if they get through, I know I'll have no problem. Another advantage to at least being second in line while riding through the forest is that I'm not the one clearing the trail of all the spider webs across the path.

To keep from getting hit by the low-hanging branch, lean forward toward your horse's neck. The first few times, your horse will take this as a clue to scoot forward faster. Take hold of the reins to stop him, so he doesn't learn to do that and make it a habit. You want him to keep up his same slow pace as you bend down to avoid the branch.

Another reason your horse might rush through the overhang is that he's naturally claustrophobic. Don't allow him to get by with it. Get off and lead him if you need to make the point. Take him through it again and again until he knows that this is a place to walk, not rush.

Branching Out

It's no fun to get hit in the head with a tree branch. When following someone through brushy or thickly forested country, stop until the person in front of you has gone through. That way you avoid getting hit with flying branches, which can actually be very dangerous to both you and your horse. You never know if the person in front of you will hold the branch until you can grab it, or if they'll let go just as you get within range. Stop and wait until that person is clear of the branch. Then it's your turn. Show the same courtesy to the person behind you. Another way to handle a branch, if possible, is to lift it.

There are times when you'll be challenged by thick overhangs in front of you, and it's easy to get knocked off. Getting under the branch can be just a matter of picking the path of least resistance. However, the trail-savvy horse can pick the best way out of this mess, usually before you can. I know that my horse looks for the best way, and he'll choose the widest opening and the tallest spot just about every time, which usually gives me plenty of room to get through. However, not all horses can judge your height as well as Max judges mine. You'll have to evaluate the best path to make it without scalping yourself.

Close Calls

Banging your knees into trees and boulders isn't fun and potentially harmful. One way to move your horse away from the tree, rock, fence or whatever the obstacle might be is to

Apply leg pressure to the horse's side to move him away from an obstacle such as this tree trunk. Here, Janine also uses her hand to push the horse away from the tree.

55

Free-swinging stirrup leathers allow you to quickly move your leg out of harm's way.

self. Over time, your horse will learn to keep away from trees and your knees will thank you.

Your saddle can play an important role in your maneuvering skills also. If a collision of your leg and an unmovable object seems to be inevitable, having free-moving stirrup leathers help you move your leg quickly to safety.

Leap of Faith

It's best to walk through ditches, deep crevices and gullies rather than jump them. With jumping, there's always the chance that your horse could land wrong or on a sharp rock or tree stump and hurt himself. However, there are times when there's no other way to get across than to jump. In doing so, take a deep seat, hold onto some mane hair to steady yourself and give your horse his head. If you hold onto the reins too tightly, you'll impede your horse's ability to get the two of you over in a smooth fashion.

Water Crossings

It's important to cross streams or rivers where the trail leads you. Look over to the other side and find the trail. As you're crossing, head toward it and don't take a shorter route unless you know the area well. There's usually a very good reason why the trail is located where it is. Don't take the chance of getting off the trail to cross water you're unfamiliar with.

A stream might have a hazardous bank that can be a real problem if your horse steps into it as he tries to get up onto the bank. If

apply typical horsemanship techniques. For example, when trying to avoid a tree trunk, apply inside leg pressure to the animal's side (the one closest to the tree) and shift your weight (same side) to the outside through your seat bones. A trained horse knows to move away from pressure and should move away from the tree.

A time-tested trick is to actually put your hand on the tree (or the rock, whatever the case may be) as you ride by and push your horse off balance, and, therefore, over a few feet. Just make sure you're going slowly enough at the time so you don't injure your-

LIFE ON THE TRAIL

Still Waters Run Deep

Once while riding in Glacier National Park in Montana, we came upon a stream that Smoke didn't want to cross. Upon first glance it looked like any other mountain stream. So, I tried to see if Max would be the first to cross. He wasn't happy about it either. The stream seemed too wide for Max and me to jump.

As Jim and I considered our options, we noticed we couldn't see the bottom of the stream. Jim got off his horse for a closer look. He stuck a long stick into the stream to get an idea of the depth, and the stick disappeared along with his elbow. The water crossing was way too deep for our horse to walk across and way too narrow to swim.

This was the only trail into the area; therefore, if we wanted to go on we had to get on the other side of the stream. For some reason, I decided to jump first – what was I thinking? Landing in the middle of a cold mountain stream wasn't a pleasant thought. However, I wanted to continue on the trail so Max and I made our attempt. What a relief when we landed on the other side safely.

Then, it was Jim and Smoke's turn. Ah, they made it! Well, Smoke's front feet made it. His back feet missed, and the next thing I knew Smoke's back legs were scrambling up the bank. But he finally got all four feet on the bank, and, after checking out the horse's legs, we were off to check out the new territory.

Look for the trail on the other side of a river or stream before you cross.

you can see into the water, it'll look different, such as a rocky stream floor that turns to a muddy looking area near the edge, where you know others haven't crossed before you. There could be a hidden rock shelf lurking under the mud or sediment, which could cause your horse to drop down several inches to several feet. If you're unfamiliar with the area, avoid getting off the trail at water crossings.

When crossing a swift running river, keep your eye on the bank on the other side and pick a rock, tree or other object to head toward. If you look down at the fast-moving water you could become dizzy and disoriented. But don't stare fixedly at the other side either. Be alert for obstacles under the water.

Downed Timber

In crossing downed timber, take your time and allow your horse to investigate where he can put his feet. It's a good rule of thumb to not step over objects higher than your horse's knee. You'll also want to watch for branches

Allow your horse to pick his way through deadfall.

Barbed-wire fences on the ground are a common occurrence, especially in areas that were once ranchland.

Wired

Whether traveling down the trail or riding across country, there's always a chance of your horse stepping into a wire that's on the ground, and barbed wire could pose a real danger to your horse. Take care when you see fence posts that don't appear to have wire attached. Old posts might have shed the wire, and it might be where your horse could step into it. There's also a common practice, in the western states mostly, of lying the wire down from the post during certain times of the years. Carrying some type of wire cutters in a saddlebag or on your belt (i.e. a leatherman tool) might be a lifesaver if your horse does get tangled in wire.

Over Hill and Dale

Whenever possible, ride into and out of steep areas at an angle. Your horse has a much better chance of not falling while traveling at a slant. If he does lose his footing, he's much more likely to slide down rather than fall. Make it a habit of crossing this way and your horse will continue to do this each time he enters a similar area.

and points sticking out of the timber that could catch you or your horse. This might be a good time to look for a way to ride around the obstacle, if it's possible.

If the deadfall is bigger than what you're comfortable with, dismount and send your horse over the obstacle. However, if you let your horse jump over downed trees all the time, then happen on one that could cause a problem, you can't expect your horse to all of a sudden not jump. It's always better to go slowly and deliberately in the beginning. After you establish your patterns, you can alter your maneuvers and your speed. Soon your horse will automatically slow down to cross a downed tree or other object.

If you travel up steep grades head on, your horse could possibly lose his footing and fall head over heels backward. Some precipitous banks might have been undercut, making them even steeper and more dangerous at the top than they appear.

Riding single file over a hill, keep a safe distance from the horse in front of you.

Hillsides are best ridden at an angle.

If you find the area too steep, find another way to go. Take a look around and pick the safest approach. You'll also want to take the footing into consideration. Take extra precaution in loose rock or slippery areas. If at all possible, avoid snow, ice and mud when traveling up- or downhill.

Visually check out the whole area you'll be covering and travel down slowly. This is especially true for the bottom on the hillside. You don't want to get almost down to the bottom only to discover that the slope has become a sudden drop-off of several feet, has a barbed wire fence or other unforeseen obstacles. If you can't see all the way to the bottom and you're unable to see a clear trail, it might be well advised to have someone walk down to check it out before you proceed on horseback. You certainly don't want to have to climb back up a steep area you wouldn't have come down if you'd scoped it out first. If you don't have a riding buddy, then perhaps you should simply find another way down.

It's wise not to run up and down hills, which can be a problem for your horse if he's out of shape and especially if the trail is a long one. Horses that tire on the trail might begin lunging up the hills. On a hazardous trail this can be extremely dangerous as your horse could easily go over backward. While running or lunging, there's a point in the horse's stride when the animal has only one hind foot on the ground and all your weight and his depend on it. It's much safer for him to have three feet on the ground, as he would in a four-beat walk, than just one, as he would in a three-beat canter or a lunging scramble.

Give the horse in front of you plenty of room. Horses sometimes become spooked by something and back up or turn around. This could be a problem for the rider right behind them if there's nowhere to escape. In fact, it's a smart idea to stop at the bottom or top of a hill and wait until the rider in front of you is safely down the trail before you proceed.

Tight Spaces

There are trails on which you'll find yourself in a quandary, seemingly with no safe place to go but back from where you came. You might be boxed in by trees or boulders on either side, or perhaps a steep hill on one side with a drop-off on the other. These predicaments only have two choices: Back up or turn your horse around.

If it's easy to back your horse, then do so carefully and slowly. However, you can't always back your horse for several feet on a narrow trail with a steep drop-off. One misstep over the side might be the beginning of a terrible experience.

Being able to turn your horse in a narrow area while mounted is a must and often the easiest way, providing you can do it safely. You'll need an agile horse to spin on a dime in a tight spot. However, some horses are like big semi trucks that need a football field to turn around in. If this is the case, you might have to dismount and back your horse on foot one inch at a time until you can find enough room to turn him.

Cliff Hanger

The edge of a cliff is a mixed bag of terror and beauty. The views can be breathtaking, but the situation can also be the most terrifying experience you'll encounter. These are the

In narrow, treacherous places, dismount and give your horse to your riding buddy. Walk up the bad part of the trail, then have your friend send your horse after you've made it to a safe spot.

kinds of places where even the bravest of us might have a problem.

Unfortunately, these kinds of trails seem to be everywhere. Some aren't as steep or deep as others, but they're all frightening. If you take your time, you can come to terms with your fear of heights. Whether it's a few feet or a few thousand feet down, the fear is the same. It's not something you manage to overcome in a short time. Don't become "fearless" when it comes to something that can be potentially dangerous. Use good common sense.

If you are afraid of heights, get off your horse, take a deep breath and walk him until you're in an area where you feel safe again. If you're unsure of what's ahead of you on the trail, dismount and tie your horse securely and walk up the trail. It's better to check out things on foot than to get you and your horse in an awkward position.

When traveling on the edge of a cliff, hill or embankment, some horses travel on the very edge of the trail, close to the drop-off, instead of the middle of the trail. Some riders actually prepare themselves to jump off if their horse should go over the edge. Without thinking, some riders lean to the inside of the trail, away from the drop-off, which in turn pushes the horse closer to the edge.

To overcome this, first you have to realize what you're doing. Evaluate the way you're sitting on your horse. Check to see if you're sitting straight and your weight is distributed evenly in the saddle. Next, learn to relax and do one of the following: Watch the trail ahead or your horse's ears or anything else to keep yourself from looking over the edge. You might also concentrate on your breathing or the sound of your horse's footfall. This will take your mind off your fear, well, maybe a little. I know it's easier said than done, but it does get easier each time you have to face this. Experience is the best teacher.

How Do You Rate?

Trails, such as those found in national forests, are often rated for their level of difficulty from easy to extremely difficult. These ratings can give you an idea of what the trail is about. They're usually fairly accurate, and if you're an experienced rider, you'll be prepared for the obstacles that might face you. However, if you're inexperienced, avoid the more complicated trails unless you're in the company of experienced riders.

If you do happen to get on a trail that's more demanding than you're used to, be very cautious. It's not a bad idea to get off and walk your horse when the footing is questionable. Your horse can balance himself much better if you aren't on his back. In fact, you could possibly throw him off balance as he tries to maneuver over a tricky place.

If an extremely difficult trail is also very narrow, such that a horse can only go forward, you might want to send a person ahead to catch the horses as they're released to handle the terrain on their own. That way you and your horse can concentrate on your footing to get through the situation safely. However, if there's a chance your horse can avoid his catcher, you and the catcher will have to be more vigilant. If possible, send others to cover any possible avenues of escape. But, be very cautions. A horse that's making his way through rough territory and looking for an escape route could be an accident waiting to happen. Don't take any chances in getting someone or your horse hurt; it's just not worth it. There's nothing better than to use some good old common sense so take the same trail back to your trailer or to another trail. The important thing is to get back safely.

Bread Crumbs

Finding your way around in most areas of the country is made fairly easy by trail markers. Trail signs vary across the country from

LIFE ON THE TRAIL
Don't Read and Ride

I was totally engrossed in the surrounding beauty as I rode down one of the trails in Montana's Lo Lo National Forest. Jim and Smoke led the way, so I took advantage of being in slow mode to check out the scenery behind me. All of a sudden I heard a thud, then a thump. I quickly turned to see Jim on the ground, Smoke standing a few feet away and a big tree branch between them. I asked Jim if he was all right, while trying to figure out what happened. Jim replied, "Yeah, I'm okay," as he rose to his feet, map in hand. I chuckled to myself as I imagined what took place. My suspicion was confirmed when he explained that it wasn't a good idea to read a map while riding. From that day on, Jim always stopped Smoke to look at a map.

It's a good idea to read maps and trail markers before heading out.

LIFE ON THE TRAIL

As the Crow Flies

The most foolproof way Jim and I have to get back to camp is our horses. Max and Smoke can find their way back to their trailer no matter where they are. We don't ride the same trails very often, so our horses are in unfamiliar territory most of the time. It never fails that they can get us back to camp, wherever that might be. There's one small detail we have to keep in mind, and that is that they like to go back "as the crow flies," which isn't always the best way to go. There have been a couple of times when we've overlooked our camp from a ridge top, which isn't the best place to be, but we were able to find an easy way to get back to camp safely.

beautifully carved wooden signs to marks cut into trees. In other areas where trees are few and far between you might find the trail to be marked with cairns (rock piles).

Trail riding is a great way to see the country, but there might not always be trail markers across the thousands of acres of countryside. Mapped trails might have faded over time as a result of weathering and non-use. However, these areas can be wonderful places to ride your horse, and they're definitely an experience worth having.

Finding your way around isn't as difficult as you might think. With maps, a compass or a global positioning system (GPS), it's much easier to find your way back to camp, so learn how to use them before you venture out. However, you should be accompanied by an experienced cross-country rider until you learn

Get off your horse and lead him through a tricky area if you think you need to for safety's sake.

the ins and outs, or, if you prefer, try short excursions until you get your bearings.

One of the best ways to keep from getting lost, however, is to study your surroundings on the outbound trip, not just when you're thinking about going back to camp or the rig. Notice the direction you're traveling and make mental notes of what you've seen. You'll be surprised at how they come into play on the return trip. Realize, though, that everything looks different when you turn around, so watch for major trail indicators, such as giant boulders or odd-shaped trees. However, this won't really help if you're riding a loop trail. In that case, maps and a compass or a GPS system come in handy.

There might be times when you find yourself in places you're not too sure of. For instance, let's say you find yourself on a steep hillside. A possible way out without going back the way you came is to look for wild animal paths or even a cattle trail. Since they have to get out of the same area, they've already done the scouting for you. Animal trails might also lead to water. Don't count on

them 100 percent, though, as they have a way of disappearing and leaving you on your own.

A word of caution: Don't go out on your first ride in an unfamiliar place late in the afternoon. This is the time when the novice might not make it back to camp before dark, and a search party is formed to look for you, if you're lucky.

The Panic Button

If you think you might be lost, it's very important not to panic. Panic is a waste of time for you and your animals. Stay calm and think about your situation.

If necessary, get off your horse, sit down with your party and discuss your options. Think about landmarks, the direction you drove into the area, other roads in the area, anything that might spark your ability to figure out where you are and what direction you should now head in. Talking it over and thinking about the situation almost always helps. You might also be able to retrace your steps. Don't be afraid to depend on your instincts and your own gut feelings. And don't forget

LIFE ON THE TRAIL

A Mad Dash

If you stop for lunch or a break and you let your horse graze, make sure you hobble him or at least keep one horse tied up. It's less likely that one of your horses will leave the other behind. However, if they decide to head back to camp without you, you'll have a horse to "head them off at the pass." It's always a long way back to camp if you have to walk. Not that I would know anything about that, of course.

Oh yes, I do remember once while riding in the Catalina State Park near Tucson, Arizona, that we had stopped for a little break and decided to let our horses munch on some green grass. After all, we'd been traveling around the country for several years, and our horses hadn't had fresh grass for years. As we sat on the ground watching the two boys enjoy their treat, all of a sudden Max and Smoke stopped eating, gazed quickly at each other, then took off simultaneously at a dead run toward camp. It was about a mile back to the horse camp and by the time we got there the campground host had unsaddled our horses, and they were munching hay in their corral. They certainly didn't seem sorry that they left us to walk back to camp.

that if you have an experienced trail horse in the group, he should be able to get you back to your rig. Just give him his head and watch him go home.

Better Safe Than Sorry

Every year horsemen and/or their horses are injured, or even worse, out on the trail. For the most part, the reasons are: not paying attention to what they're doing, riding an unconditioned horse or being out of riding shape themselves, venturing beyond their skill level, traveling too fast through a hazardous area or letting their ego get the best of them by taking stupid chances. Don't let this happen to you. Think about what you're doing at all times and be prepared.

If you're riding a young or inexperienced horse, do your trail riding with more seasoned horses and riders. Even if you pony him while you're out trail riding, this gives the novice horse the chance to learn from pros.

If at any point during a ride you feel uncomfortable, get off and walk. If the task is beyond your experience, don't take a chance of getting yourself or your horse hurt. Your skills will improve with your experience level. Take your time and go slowly. It's not worth pushing yourself or your horse beyond your capabilities.

Keep 'em Open

At many trailheads you'll find either cards or sheets of paper for names and comments. It's important you sign the comment sheets and let the governmental agency that's responsible for the trail know you're riding horses. These comments are used in a lot of places to determine trail usage. If riders aren't using it enough, they might decide to close it to horsepeople. Unfortunately, this happens all over the country, so let your voice be heard. Sign the cards!

8 TRAILERS AND HAULING DOWN THE ROAD

When it comes to camping with horses, trailering rig options are limitless.

The "livability" of horse trailers has grown immensely over the years along with the increasing population of traveling horse-men. There was a time when traveling to your favorite trailhead for a camping weekend was limited to vans, slide-in truck campers, homemade trailer facilities and tents. Now, living quarters horse trailers are a great home-away-from-home for many trail riders.

However, when considering any hauling rig, weight, width and length are important factors that should weigh in your decision. Most trail-heads, campgrounds and narrow roads were developed long before the big rigs came along and many aren't conducive to maneuverability. A truck with a slide-in camper pulling a two-horse trailer might be the wisest choice in the long run to avoid the length issue.

Living Quarters Trailers

On the other hand, living quarters trailers come in a variety of lengths to suit any size requirement, from small, barebones, economy-model "weekender" units with a bed, bath and minimal cooking facilities to 50-plus feet of luxurious living space, with wood floors, maple cabinetry, ovens, barbecue grills, satellite tele-visions and plush upholstery, costing hundreds of thousands of dollars. The latter is much more suited to the show scene than the back-country, so choose wisely and don't become amenity-blind when you ogle the big rigs at the trailer dealership.

If your trailer's living area is your focal point, though, you might want to think about going wider rather than longer. An 8-foot wide trailer or perhaps a sliding extension off the main living area could give you adequate space. Your towing rig will be much easier to handle driving through cities or winding coun-try roads with a shorter trailer.

Weight is probably the most underesti-mated consideration in buying rigs. Remember the bigger the trailer, the heavier, and more truck you'll need to haul the mon-ster. Many of the big rigs are safely towed only by semi-trucks or oversized truck conversions. You'll also need to be aware of ground clear-ance when taking your rig off the main high-ways so you don't destroy any of the tanks and pipes that are unprotected under your rig. Your trailer should be either high enough off the ground and/or have skid plates welded to the bottom as protection from rough roads and rocks that threaten that area.

There are pros and cons to steel verses alu-minum trailers. Steel is less expensive than aluminum, but the biggest consideration is weight, which affects the truck size you'll need to pull the heavy load. Many large trail-ers require an expensive diesel hauler to

Narrow backcountry roads can make getting to your destination with a long rig a real challenge.

LIFE ON THE TRAIL

Tight Squeeze

Jim and I once spent the summer as campground hosts at a horse camp near Sisters, Oregon. The developed sites were dispersed along the tree line and were accessed by a circular drive in the center of the camp. The inside circle was surrounded by a board fence. As folks drove around the gravel drive to a site, the longer rigs had to be extremely careful not to hit the fence as they maneuvered into the site. Unfortunately, not everyone was successful. I wish I had a dollar for every scratch, bump, lost headlight, taillight and knocked-down fence rails that occurred that summer. I'd be rich!

accommodate the weight. Therefore, if you're considering a steel trailer because of the cost factor, and you want all the amenities in your living quarters, you certainly might have to step up in weight and engine power with your towing vehicle.

Motor Homes

Motor homes have grown in popularity as a trail rider's lodging, while they tow the horse's home along behind. Motor homes come in three main categories: class A, class C and the diesel pusher. Class A's are the classic-style motor homes, smooth rectangular shape, where the driving compartment is actually a part of the living quarters. Class C motor

Campers on trucks hauling bumper-pull trailers are a favorite way to live with horses on the road.

homes have the front end of a truck van or pickup truck, with the overhang much like that of a slide-in truck camper. The driver's compartment isn't an integral part of the living facilities. Diesel pushers or coaches, as they are known, are the top of the line of the motor homes and usually 40-plus feet long.

If you prefer a motor home, you've a couple of choices about hauling your horse trailer. One is to haul it behind your motor home. If you do this, it's very important to know that the motor, transmission, frame construction, gear ratio, braking system and towing capacity are adequate to handle a loaded horse trailer.

The other choice involves two people – one driving the motor home and the other pulling the trailer with a pickup truck. The advantages of the latter option are that you have a very roomy place to live, and with the pickup, you can get to most trailheads to ride your horses.

LIFE ON THE TRAIL

Marital Bliss

Hooking up your tow vehicle to your trailer is the cause of a lot of matrimonial strife in the horse community. Men and women look at his procedure totally differently. Men know there's a standard way of signaling to the driver which way the hookup person wants him to go. Women, who're usually the ones giving the directions, know there's a simpler way of doing it. The best way to do it, without a doubt, is the way the woman wants. The man does the backing and she'll do the signaling, telling him which way to go. In the interest of nuptial harmony, the couple should review the signals before starting to actually hook up the rig. Works for me.

Plus, with the pickup you can travel into town for supplies or dinner and not have to find a parking lot for a behemoth motor home. This is a viable choice if you want to spend a lot of time on the road and travel around the country. However, your fuel bills might be prohibitive as you have to pay for both vehicles.

Truck Campers

Slide-in truck campers, the SUV of camping, are very popular with the trail riding set, especially in the western states. A slide-in truck camper in the back of your four-wheel-drive pickup pulling a two- or three-horse trailer can get you to just about any trailhead. Slide-in campers have come a long way in design and amenities. Some even have a slide-out extension to give you more usable space.

Some of the newer models are equipped with remote control jacks, making the process of getting the camper on and off your truck a real snap. It's possible to take the camper off while you're visiting an area, and use your truck without the camper. A plus to the slide-in is that it doesn't have wheels, which means that you don't have to buy a license tag for it.

Other Choices

I'm always impressed with the talent and imagination some people have when it comes to their accommodations, such as converting stock/horse trailers into their living facilities when they arrive at their destination. Turning moving vans and buses into viable horse and people transporters and camping facilities are wonderful ways to fulfill your traveling needs. And, of course, tents are always in fashion and within anyone's budget. Where there's a will there's a way.

A Weighty Matter

When you're selecting your trailer, remember, the larger it is, the bigger and more powerful the tow vehicle must be. We've all seen a pickup truck pulling a 20,000-plus-pound living quarters trailer. The truck's engine might be adequate enough to pull the trailer but, the vehicle's brakes aren't always capable of stopping that much weight.

Overloading your trailer can have a multitude of repercussions, but the main one is that you won't have the ability to stop the vehicle. This is critical when you're traveling down a steep grade, and find you're actually being "pushed" down the hill by your own trailer, often referred to as the "the tail wagging the dog."

Your braking system's capability is in direct relationship to the weight limits and ranges of your tow vehicle, so heed the recommendations from the manufacturer. It can negate the warranty on your tow vehicle if you happen to encounter engine or transmission problems because of the overloading issue.

It's incumbent upon you to find out what your tow rig's weight capacity is, as well as that of your trailer. Don't take someone's word unless you know he's an expert in this field. It's your responsibility to know what you're driving and hauling. Find out from your vehicle and trailer manufacturer what the towing capacity is for each.

The automobile and trailer industries have done exhaustive testing of their products and have made the weight limitations based on safety and equipment capacities. Overloading isn't only destructive to your equipment, but also unsafe for you, your horse and others on the road. And, if you have an accident with an overloaded rig, you can be held liable no matter what the circumstances might have been.

Most of us tend to pack more things and supplies than we really need. If you put a little thought into your real needs, you can leave a lot of your belongings back home and help cut back on the weight. If you're going to be gone on a long trip, you can cut the amount of feed and hay you carry in the trailer and re-supply when you arrive at your destination. This same line of thinking goes for the amount of canned goods and supplies that can just as easily be bought in the local area. Wait to fill your water tanks, as well, but be certain you've enough for your own needs and the horses.

Another heavy issue is fuel. If you're traveling through the mountains you might not want to totally fill up your tank until you're through the tough grades. Just make sure there's a town on the other side so you can fuel up again.

Carrying large objects on the outside of your trailer, either on top or fastened to the sides, can interfere with wind resistance and be detrimental to your fuel mileage. Also, keep in mind that carrying heavy things on the tongue of your trailer increases the tongue weight on your tow vehicle. Check your owner's manual to see if you're within your limits.

Safety Issues

There are numerous considerations and modifications that might make your hauling safer, such as modifying trailer hitches, adding engine

Sideview mirrors allow you to see your trailer and the road behind you.

LIFE ON THE TRAIL

Back in the 1980s there weren't many horse folks traveling across the country to ride. But, what did we know? All we wanted was to ride in the Rocky Mountains. So we loaded up our old Class C motor home, put our three horses in our stock trailer and off we went. Jim, our youngest son Clint and I drove across the country, stopping along the way to ride our horses as we journeyed west.

Things went fairly smoothly until we headed up Monarch Pass in Colorado. Little did we know that this pass is one of the highest in the state. With all the weight we were carrying, since we brought everything that we could think of and then some, our motor home vapor-locked. We had to pull over to the side of the road every mile or so to let the engine cool down.

At one stop, a man came up to Jim, and, after hearing our story, made some suggestions. Well, they were worth a try.

Inside our motor home was a cover to the engine compartment, called the engine cowl, which the man recommended we remove. We again started up the 11,000-plus-foot mountain. As we climbed, Jim turned on the heater, as if all the heat from the engine coming through that huge opening wasn't enough. To cool ourselves off, we rolled down the windows.

We continued driving up the mountain without any more stops, with one exception. We had to find a stick that Jim could use to hold down the accelerator when the heat on his leg became unbearable.

We finally made it to the summit and soon were going down the other side, heading toward our destination. Our engine cooled off and our flared tempers, too.

Although this was not the only snag on our maiden voyage, it was all part of the continuing education that taught us a great deal about traveling with horses.

LIFE ON THE TRAIL

Highway Leapfrog

I must say that I don't believe I'll ever be comfortable driving a rig through a big city. Cars and trucks buzz by me like I'm standing still, and I'm doing the speed limit! And why is it that no matter how hard I try to keep a big enough space between me and the driver ahead of me, another car always gets between us? I have to give up more space to him, and then another car gets between us. It's just a never-ending story of some strange game of leapfrog. Guess they went to a different school of driving than I did.

Rubber bumpers make entering and exiting the trailer safer for your horse.

retarders and using equalizer hitches and anti-sway bars for bumper-pull horse trailers. There are many ways of doing things, lots of "tricks of the trade," and people who are knowledgeable in these areas. With a little research and talking to manufacturers, you can find the right safety equipment for your particular rig.

Safety, of course is the most important consideration in deciding about your tow vehicle and trailer. You want to ask a lot of questions, call the manufacturer and read all the literature you can find. You need to learn all you can in order to make an educated decision.

The Art of Driving

Driving a rig is a huge responsibility. There's much more to the process than getting in, starting the engine and driving off down the road. You should always be aware of the fact that there's a trailer behind you, and the safety and wellbeing of your animals are in your hands. There are actually drivers who never look back at the trailer during their whole trip. How do they know if it's still there?

Driving a rig takes concentration and skill to maneuver on and off the highway. Having a good set of side mirrors on your vehicle is a must. Not only can you see the traffic behind you but you also can keep an eye on your trailer. Keeping your rig between the highway lines is very important and side mirrors can help you judge your distance. You don't want trailer wheels to drop off the edge of the road. It's not always an easy task to determine if your trailer tires have gone flat or even blown out while on the road, making it a good idea to be able to glance at your trailer tires in the mirrors.

Be careful of how you make corners with any rig, but especially a long one. Swing wide at a corner so that the back end of your trailer won't run over the curb or hit a stop sign or fence post. Narrow streets, parking lots and gas stations can be treacherous if you're not careful in how you maneuver through parked cars, curbs and gas pumps.

Driving in hilly country and especially in mountainous regions can be tough on your rig. When driving in these areas, don't overuse the brakes. Excessive braking can wear them out quickly and/or they might overheat to a point of making them virtually useless. These are conditions you don't want anytime, let alone while traveling steep hills and mountains. The best way to slow your vehicle in these conditions is through the transmission. Shifting down to a lower gear is much safer and easier on your vehicle. That way you can apply your brakes sparingly. Another good option is using your trailer brake to slow you down before putting on your vehicle brakes. In many instances, this might be all you need to reduce your speed. You won't have to use the brakes at all, thus saving them for when you need to stop or in an emergency.

Backing your rig can be a little tricky. It's wise to learn the technique at home or in a big parking lot before you take off on your trip. It can be very frustrating to be in a position where you have to back up and you become the center of attention. It's not much fun to have the added pressure of onlookers or having several people trying to tell you different ways of proceeding. Skip this part of a hard lesson and learn how to do it before you encounter the "backing" spectacular. And don't forget to use your side mirrors!

LIFE ON THE TRAIL

Ding-Dong

Talk about not paying attention to your surroundings while you're driving! We know of a couple who, upon their arrival at their destination, discovered that their trailer was missing. They had no idea when they lost it or where the trailer, or their horses, could be. They were extremely lucky when they back-tracked their route and found the trailer parked in an open field where it'd come to rest. The horses were unharmed inside the trailer and busily munching away on hay.

Rest Stops

Stopping every couple of hours for fuel, a restroom break or to eat allows you to relax and stretch your legs. This works well for most people, and it gives the horses a chance to relax, too. Having to stand up in a moving trailer is work for them. This is a good time to offer your horses a drink of water or give them some hay. Open up all the trailer windows and allow your horses to hang their heads out if they can. This also provides air circulation.

Some people take their horses out of the trailer to exercise, but this isn't always necessary and might even be dangerous. The biggest problem is simply finding a safe place to do it. Many developed rest stops have lush, green grass lawns surrounding them, and your horse will want to nibble. I'm sure you've noticed, though, that this beautiful grass is weed-free, and there's a good reason for that. It's not a good idea to have your horse munch on grass that's been sprayed with weed killers and other chemicals.

What happens if your horse gets spooked and runs away? Traffic and other distractions can be very confusing to horses. Even the best of them can do silly things and put themselves and others in danger. You also run the risk of your horse not wanting to get back into the trailer. You have to ask yourself if a little exercise is worth all the potential problems.

Offer water to your horses at every rest stop.

When you stop for any reason, open the trailer windows for your horses' comfort.

LIFE ON THE TRAIL

Rope Tricks

We'd been driving about eight hours to get to our destination. When we arrived, the wind was blowing, it was bitter cold, raining and just plain miserable. There was nowhere at the campground for the horses to get in out of the weather, so we decided to leave them in the trailer. It happened to be the very first trip for them in their new trailer, but everything seemed to be going well.

The next morning we got an early start on the day's drive ahead of us. At our first gas station stop there happened to be an open field next to the station. Feeling sorry for the horses, we decided to let them out of the trailer to stretch their legs, after asking permission from the store owner first, of course. The horses seemed to be more interested in eating the grass than getting some exercise.

After about a half hour we decided it was time to get back on the road. Smoke loaded up as usual. Max, for the first and only time ever, refused to get into the trailer. I circled him and circled him and circled him, to no avail. We tried grain, carrots, more grain, anything and everything that we could think of. What a nightmare.

After an hour, I was totally drained, completely out of ideas and on the verge of tears. Alas! Our hero pulled up behind us in his pickup truck and saved the day. After hearing the story of our plight, he performed a few rope tricks on Max, smacked him on the behind and we had our horse once more in the trailer. After that, we never left him in the trailer overnight again.

9 FINDING PLACES TO STAY AND RIDE

Some incredible sights can be found in our nation's backcountry, on both public and private lands. These riders, who are marveling at cliff dwellings and petroglyphs, had to have a Navajo guide to escort them into Canyon de Chelly National Monument, which belongs to the Navajo Nation.

You might be amazed at the number of places there are in this country to ride your horse. If you take the time to do a little research you can literally find thousands of places to choose from. At one point during our travels, I was keeping a database of places to ride. This wasn't just a list of trails, but trailheads (places with numerous trails leaving from one point) or access points to different trails, such as state parks, national forest campgrounds, etc. I literally found more than 6,000 places to ride and I was still finding more. So, what are you waiting for?

Whose Land is it?

Riding opportunities occur on either public or private land. Public land includes national, state and regional parks and national and state forests. Private land is typically farm or ranchland that you must receive the owner's permission to ride on.

Educate yourself on what's available in the governmental agencies and their rules. This also makes your traveling easier, although it's not possible to know all the rule changes and variations of agencies in the different states. Nevertheless, knowledge is power, as they say, and having even the slightest idea of what's acceptable in an area might just help you find a place to camp and ride.

National agencies usually have a great number of trails for the horseman. This is particularly true for the western states. National forests, parks, recreational areas and the Bureau of Land Management (BLM) lands are great places to ride. Trails are very prevalent although they might not be marked. There are lots of opportunities for cross-country riding, via a vast trail network, providing never-ending adventures for you and your equine partner.

Not all national agencies are alike; they're run by different departments of the government. The National Forest Service is under the umbrella of the Department of Agriculture, while the National Park Service and BLM are run by the Department of the Interior. Rules, fees and facilities differ.

State and county agencies have numerous parks and forest land that might have trails for your recreation. However, they typically don't have as many as national agencies, and they frequently have more rules, and less chance for cross-country riding.

Private facilities, usually more prevalent in the East and Midwest, normally offer great camping amenities and lots of riding on private land, as well as access to public lands. By and large, they're more costly than state and national facilities; however, the accommodations are generally better.

Who're You Going to Call?

For handy reference, carry a list of addresses and phone numbers for national forest, BLM, state agencies and their district offices. When you're in a new area, stop by or call the district office for info on where you can camp, even if you've called, e-mailed or written ahead of time, as road and weather conditions, water

National forests and other public lands have many rules and regulations, such as those posted on trailhead bulletin boards, you should be aware of before heading into the backcounty.

Let your fingers do the walking and look in phone books for the names of local stables who can put your horses up for the night.

availability, forest fires and many other circumstances change rapidly. Whether you need a place to stay for the night or a place to ride and camp for an extended period of time, most districts can give you that information. It's also a good idea to let the officials know you're there.

As you're traveling through an area, particularly a town or city, it might be prudent to stop at a pay phone to find a place to stay. You can look in the phone directory to see if there's a fairgrounds, stable or other places that might be able to put your horse up for the night.

Another good place for information is at a feed store, tack shop or a equine veterinary clinic. They're familiar with the area and might have some ideas where you can keep your horse.

Some rigs and roads don't mesh.

All the Right Questions

Back roads can be a little tricky to follow if you're not used to them. They're a lot different than the well-marked highways in urban areas, so know exactly where you're going and if you can actually get to your destination. This is especially true if you're going into the backcountry or a very rural area.

When you stop at the government or trail facility's office, there'll be someone there who can help answer your questions. If this person isn't familiar with the roads, trails and the area you're going to, ask to speak to someone else, preferably the person who manages the actual trails. If this person isn't available, you'll want to speak to a person who rides or at least hikes in the area. If you haven't been to the area before, you don't know what you might be getting into on the roads to the camp or trailhead.

When you find the right person, ask the right questions, those that can keep you out of trouble and as safe as possible. If it's at all possible, take this person outside the office so he/she can see your rig, and ask, "Can I get this rig safely down the road and to the campground or the trailhead?" You want the person to be fully aware of what you're driving. There've been numerous times we were told we could get our rig somewhere, only to find out the hard way we couldn't!

If you find yourself in doubt about a road you're on, park your rig, get out and walk or unload your horses and ride the unknown road. This might sound like a lot of trouble, but it's better than getting into a real mess with your rig. If you've ever had to back up your rig several miles on a narrow, curvy back road, you won't mind this little inconvenience.

Another question to ask before you start your journey to the trailhead is if there's any potable water and water for the horses. You don't want to drive miles only to find there's no water. If you ask before you leave, you have the opportunity to take adequate water with you.

Ask what wild animals are native to the area. Although you'll probably never see them, it's good to know if there are poisonous snakes, mountain lions or bears in the area. If you know what's out there, you can be prepared, such as keeping your food put away so you won't invite animals into your camp.

LIFE ON THE TRAIL

You're Going Where?

A government district office sent us out on a very narrow, one-lane mountain road. Luckily, before we'd gotten too far, we ran into a local rancher, who asked where we were planning to camp. When we told him our plans, he actually gasped. He told us that we'd never get our rig down that road. He suggested that we stop before going much farther, while we still had some open space to turn around, and walk down the road to check it out. We took his advice, parked our rig and walked down the road. The very steep road was in itself scary, not to mention that on one side of the road there was a drop-off of several hundred feet. The other side had a rock overhang with about a six-foot clearance, not nearly enough to get our rig under.

If you can't see what's around a treacherous corner, get out of your vehicle and take a look.

Know the Rules

There are some areas of the country where government employees aren't used to dealing with horse travelers and their equipment. They simply don't know how to deal with folks who want to do something out of their area of expertise or comfort zone. It's incumbent upon you to understand this and to deal with these kinds of situations rather than looking to others to solve your dilemmas.

If you're aware of the customary rules used elsewhere, you might be able to clarify the procedures for the person in charge. For example, if you want to camp in a regular forest service campground and the host only knows that horses aren't allowed in the campground, you can explain that the usual practice of other forest service campgrounds is to place horses outside the boundary of the camp. This usually gets the positive response you're looking for.

However, never assume that, because you know the rules for the national forest in your state, those rules apply to all other states. That's not always the case. You could spoil your vacation fast when, after a long day's drive, you can't find a place to camp or ride.

Usually the rules and regulations are the same within the state, but they can vary from state to state. Rules are usually up for interpretation, so how the person in control interprets the rules is how they'll be enforced.

The Hassles

When you learn to anticipate what might be in store for you, you might just be able to save yourself some hassles.

Here's a common scenario. Let's say you're planning a day ride into a national park. Call ahead to find out if there are any special requirements. If they require you to feed your horse weed-free hay 48 hours before entering the park and you didn't know to do that, there could be some hitches in your plans. Park officials might not allow you to ride until you comply with the rules, or they might ask you to pick up and remove your horse's manure while you ride. It's much better to have fed your horse weed-free hay ahead of time rather than to spend your ride paying attention to your horse's droppings.

Unfortunately there are a few hassles out there for the trail rider. But they in no way compare to the countless hours of pleasure

Weather and road conditions can change rapidly. Know what you're getting into before you go. This road was flooded out the day before.

that are waiting for you. So don't let a few minor details keep you from seeing this beautiful country from the back of your horse.

Volunteering

Trail riders who're looking for unique experiences in finding places to stay and ride might want to explore the idea of volunteering or hosting. Opportunities exist all over the country. Whether you want to stay close to home or travel to a new region, performing this function could be an interesting and rewarding way to add a new chapter to your summer vacation or winter getaway.

National agencies such as the Bureau of Land Management, National Forest Service and the National Park Service have very strong volunteer programs. State, county, and city parks might also be possibilities. The NFS has a program called the U.S. National Forest Volunteer Program. Contact the Forest Service's regional office, BLM office, National Park or state agency for the area where you want to work. Write or call the volunteer coordinator at the specific park in which you would like to volunteer and ask how you can help.

Horse patrols are popular in state parks. Volunteers ride their horses on the park's trails, observing and reporting trail use and conditions back to those in charge. They're also a big help in assisting visitors by answering

LIFE ON THE TRAIL

A Pair of Pros

A few years ago we had the opportunity to meet a couple of young ladies who were volunteering out of the Bend/Fort Rock Ranger District of the Deschutes National Forest in Oregon. In camp they conducted educational talks to all the trail users. As we rode the trails with them, we were very impressed with the ease with which they handled all situations. We watched as they calmly explained to a father the dangers of his child shooting a BB gun so close to a horse and hiking trail; they were inspiring at a trailhead where children had gathered to pet the horses; they were very entertaining as they interacted with a group of hikers along the trail and very persistent as they cleaned up old, neglected backcountry camp sites. These young ladies presented a very professional persona, from their official uniform to their wealth of information and obvious dedication.

questions, handing out maps and informing visitors of the parks rules and regulations.

A backcountry or wilderness ranger volunteer might perform actual patrols in the backcountry. Duties could include checking the condition of the trails and maintaining them, making contact with visitors, answering questions and teaching "Leave No Trace" skills and ethics. These volunteer positions are growing in number throughout the Western states. With the reduction of staff, due to budget cuts and an increase in visitors, volunteers are very much appreciated.

Campground host positions at horse camps are plentiful across the country. Responsibilities vary from park to park but, typically they could be things such as: greeting campers, answering questions, explaining the rules and regulations (not enforcing them) and perhaps replenishing restroom supplies. In exchange for your services, in addition to learning new skills and having a new outdoor experience, you might also receive a free campsite.

Facilities vary from having a paved RV pad with electricity, water and telephone while your horse enjoys a stall or paddock to a primitive site nestled in a grove of trees by a pristine stream, dirt or gravel camping pad, pole corrals and a picnic table.

Campground hosts are usually selected on a first-come, first-served basis. However, if the open position happens to be in a well-liked hosting area, where being a host is very popular, other criteria might apply. This could include your camping knowledge, prior campground host experiences, skills working with the public and the length of time you're willing to be a host.

10 THE TRIP

Planning a trip with friends doubles the fun.

The distance from your home to you riding destination can seem like an eternity at times. Because they're so special to us, we'd all like our vacations or adventures to go off without a hitch. Unfortunately, life doesn't always work that way. If you look at the whole situation in realistic terms rather than in the way you'd like for it to go, life can be a lot easier on you and the people around you.

Here are some important things you'll need to consider in planning your trip and some tips to make the trip more enjoyable and lessen the stress.

Interstate Travel

Traveling around the country with your horses can be a wonderful experience; however, crossing state lines can be a complicated process. Trying to figure out which states require what documents is a real headache. To make life a little easier, here's some insight into the world of interstate horse-traveling.

There are at least two separate documents required by every state among the necessary paperwork you'll need to cross state lines. The Certificate of Veterinary Inspection, commonly known as a health certificate, is a must-have for all traveling horsemen. It's valid for 30 days, and on it your veterinarian will describe your horse and his markings, note where the horse is going to be transported and by whom, check your horse for signs of illness or disease and list the Coggins test results (see below.)

The other required paperwork is a test for the viral disease equine infectious anemia (EIA), also known as swamp fever, malarial fever, mountain fever or slow fever. The Coggins test, which is proof that your equine has tested negative for the disease, must have

A typical Certificate of Veterinary Inspection describes the horse, gives the Coggins test results and the owner's information, in addition to noting where the horse is being shipped.

The Coggins certificate depicts the horse and its markings and notes the accession number of the laboratory blood test.

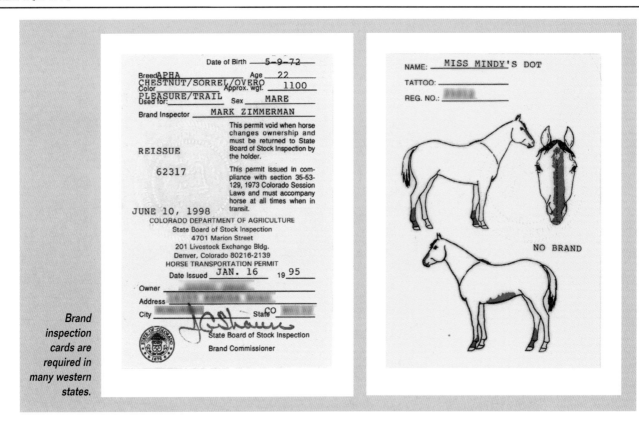

Date of Birth ___5-9-72___

Breed __APHA__ Age __22__
Color __CHESTNUT/SORREL/OVERO__ Approx. wgt. __1100__
Used for: __PLEASURE/TRAIL__ Sex __MARE__

Brand Inspector ___MARK ZIMMERMAN___

REISSUE

62317

This permit void when horse changes ownership and must be returned to State Board of Stock Inspection by the holder.

This permit issued in compliance with section 35-53-129, 1973 Colorado Session Laws and must accompany horse at all times when in transit.

JUNE 10, 1998

COLORADO DEPARTMENT OF AGRICULTURE
State Board of Stock Inspection
4701 Marion Street
201 Livestock Exchange Bldg.
Denver, Colorado 80216-2139
HORSE TRANSPORTATION PERMIT
Date Issued __JAN. 16__ 19__95__

Owner _____
Address _____
City _____ State __CO__

State Board of Stock Inspection
Brand Commissioner

NAME: ___MISS MINDY'S DOT___
TATTOO: _____
REG. NO.: _____

NO BRAND

Brand inspection cards are required in many western states.

been performed in the six months prior to your departure, or the past year, depending on the state's requirement. You must present this document with the health certificate when crossing state lines, as well as at most stables, campgrounds and public riding areas. Visit your veterinarian far in advance of your departure date; it could take weeks to get the results back from a Coggins blood test.

Some states have reciprocal agreements. Oregon and Washington, for example, exempt each other's equines from the EIA tests. However, other requirements might apply. For instance, some states require that the horse's temperature be recorded on the CVI.

Brand Inspection

As you travel west of the Mississippi River, it gets a little more complicated. In addition to a current Coggins test and health certificate, you might need brand inspection papers for all horses in your trailer, depending on the particular western state's laws.

Ownership inspection, sometimes called "brand inspection" or "hauling papers," is required when leaving certain states. Brand inspections harken back to the open range days, when a rancher had to prove which livestock belonged to him by having his brand somewhere on the animal. Most horses these days aren't physically branded. Instead, the

inspection paperwork indicates colors, white markings, scars, swirls, etc., to help identify individual horses.

The state brand inspector is required to physically inspect the animal and you must show proof of ownership at that time. The inspector draws the horse's distinctive marks on an outline, examines the horse's registration papers or bill of sale, and/or takes your statement that the horse is your own. After paying a fee per animal, you'll be given a certificate or laminated card.

Brand inspections can be obtained as either an annual or a lifetime inspection and are valid until the horse changes ownership. If you travel frequently with your horses, you'll probably want to get the lifetime inspection.

If you're hauling a horse for a friend, you'll need all the same paperwork in hand to show state officials.

Interstate Equine Passport

The Passport Health Certificate or the Passport is similar to the regular health certificate, in that it has an accurate drawing of all horse's markings and brands, but it is good for six months and can be used for unlimited travel in the states covered. Like the 30-day certificate, you'll need the permanent or annual brand inspection certificate number, a tattoo, brand or microchip implant and the

LIFE ON THE TRAIL

Murphy's Law

On one trip to the West, we'd made arrangement to stay at a stable in Kansas. We were traveling with folks who were uncomfortable not knowing where they would be staying. That turned out to be prophetic. The stable owners didn't give us directions, saying the place was difficult to find. They told us to call when we got into town; they'd meet us and we could follow them back to their place. We called, but there was no answer and no answering machine.

We asked around town and no one had ever heard of the stable. We flagged down a city policeman and his reply was the same – never heard of them.

We tried calling the stable again. This time someone who worked at the stable answered, but he told us that he didn't know how to get there. Duh!

We stopped at a local store and asked directions to the fairgrounds. When we got there, we discovered that the gate was locked. So, back to town where we were given a phone number for the man who should have the key, then back to the fairgrounds to wait, and wait and wait some more. We did finally make it into the fairgrounds and things went much better the next day.

Coggins test results. The owner's name, address and phone number must be provided, as well as the name and stabling address of the horse. A traveling permit number must be obtained by telephone from each state that's involved. The phone numbers are provided on the Passport form.

The only drawback to having this Passport form is you have to keep an itinerary of the interstate travel for that individual horse. Then, within 10 days after the six month expires, a copy showing both sides of the Passport must be mailed to the state veterinarian of each state you entered. However, if you travel to any other state with your horse that's not on the list, you'll have to purchase a regular 30-day health certificate to enter that state.

Stopping at State Lines

There are times when it's confusing about what you should do when you see a sign saying "agriculture stop," "weigh station," "Port of Entry" or "all vehicles hauling livestock must stop." If you see a sign that says anything about agriculture, stop, and, if asked, show all your paperwork. You usually don't need to stop at a regular truck weigh station. However, if you're in doubt, then stop. That's better than being chased down by a patrol officer.

This all might seem to be a bit of a hassle, and you might think it's hardly worth the trouble. Just remember that if you're stopped without correct papers, you can be given a hefty fine and your horses and rig can be impounded. That would put a real damper on your trip.

Also, realize that states might change their policies and entry requirements at any time. Stay on top of this and be prepared. With the increase in horsemen traveling around the country, states are becoming more strict and aware of their responsibility to keep their livestock as safe and free of disease as possible.

The United State Department of Agriculture has the latest regulations on interstate movement of animals. You can find the information and phone numbers on the Internet. For clarification on any of the rules and regulations, contact the state veterinarian office of any state you want to visit or travel through. This also can be found on the Internet, or you can call a toll free number: 800-545-8732.

Planning Your Trip

If traveling with your horse is new to you, plan to make your first trip short. After you've decided where you want to go, get out the maps. Locate your destination, and figure out how far it is from home. Then decide how far you want to travel in a day, giving consideration to how much time you've allocated for your trip. Do you want to take your time getting there and enjoy the region in between home and your destination, or do you want to just get there and spend the bulk of your time riding in your chosen location?

Once you decide, then it's time to look at your maps again. If you're traveling about 400 miles to your destination, then on the map about 350 miles from home, locate an available place to stay the night — a large city, forest or park. Also, decide if you want to stay in the area to ride or just stay for the night.

Remote BLM lands are usually worth the trouble to find, but some require permits for camping.

A designated trailhead close to a paved road is a real treat.

Information Please

You can find information to help you formulate your plans in many places, which will be evident by the stacks of paper you'll accumulate. Send postcards, letters or e-mails to various areas of the country. Some good sources include state and city tourist bureaus and city chambers of commerce. Explain that you'll be traveling to their area with your horses and request information on trails, horse facilities, camping, regulations, fees and anything else you think might pertain to that particular area of the country.

Although most places do respond, the information they send might be a surprise. Some of the information you'll receive will make you question if they even bothered to read your request. Others will be extremely detailed and reveal how people have gone out of their way to mark maps, showing you where to find trailheads, camping and even the best town to restock your supplies.

As mentioned in the last chapter, one of the first places to request information is the U.S. Forest Service. National forests in most states have endless trails and lots of camping opportunities (often primitive). However, there are some national forests that have excellent facilities.

Addresses for national forest offices can be found in a variety of places. In addition to Web sites on the Internet, you'll find that libraries and bookstores have a diverse selection of books on the USFS. You can also obtain addresses from your nearby forest service office. It's a good idea to write to all the ranger districts within the area in which you're going to travel. That way you can cover all of your options. In case one place doesn't offer what you want, one of the others might.

Bureau of Land Management areas are also good places to look into, especially in the western states. You can usually camp and ride anywhere on BLM lands, although some districts might require permits; be sure to check. You might also find an occasional campground.

Many national parks have some fantastic riding areas that a lot of people overlook. Even though national parks usually have some trails or roads for the equestrian, unfortunately most don't offer camping or have facilities for horses. They might require a permit to ride within the park, so check with the park office. The national parks that do offer camping and horse facilities usually require reservations. These parks are popular so call in advance of your arrival date. You have a better chance of getting into these places from Monday through Thursday. You might also be able to get in at the last minute because of a cancellation. So don't give up hope on a popular spot.

National Recreational Areas are another place to write for information. Some have great trails and horse facilities. If your dream is to ride on a beach, you can check into an area in which you would like to ride. Some areas open their beaches during the winter months for horseback riding. Don't forget to check into national seashores for their riding season.

Many state parks and state forests offer horseback riding and camping. Some have great facilities including electric, water, level trailer pads and showers.

Other areas to explore are U.S. Corps of Engineers lands, city and municipal parks, national battlefields, wildlife management areas, military installations and Rails-to-Trails. Information can also be found in books, magazines and if you have a computer, don't forget the Internet.

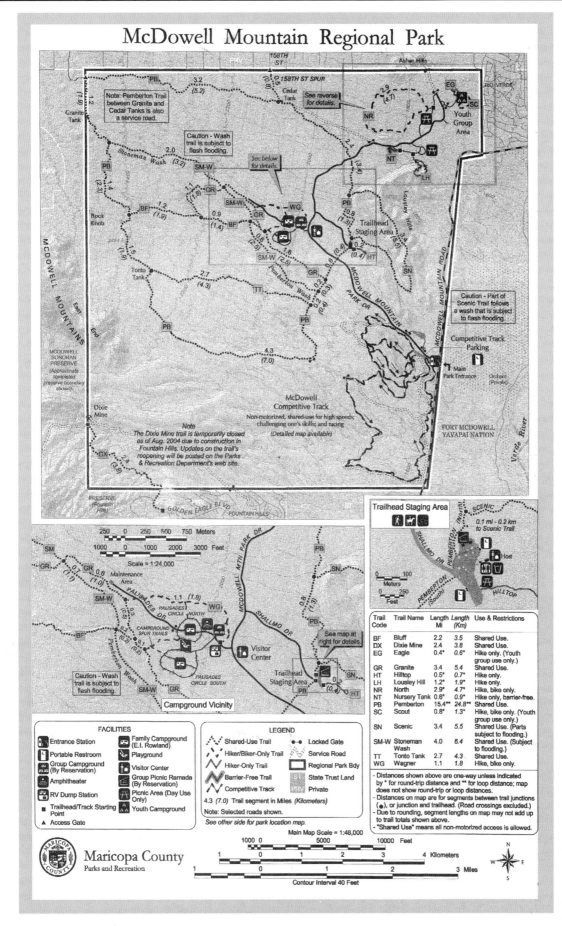

McDowell Mountain Regional Park

Detailed maps of the trails you plan to ride come in handy when planning your trips.

You'll find that the more you travel and the more people you meet, the more places you'll find to ride. Another good source, especially for the eastern states, is the American Horse Council's Horse Industry Directory. Here you can find information about state horse councils and riding groups that might be of help to you.

Other good sources for information are phone books. They can be found at your local library or on the Internet. They include listings for national, state, city and county facilities. There's just a world of information for each area. You can also find veterinarians, feed stores, stables, horse motels and fairgrounds for that particular area. Don't forget to look on state highway maps as some states list their parks and activities.

Always make alternate plans for wherever you're planning to stay or ride. So many things can happen or go wrong on a trip that it can be mind-boggling. The length of the trip, the weather, the number of people, horses and rigs can all increase the number of things that can go wrong. You might simply be disappointed with your accommodations and want to make an early exit. You could be sitting at the side of the road, twiddling your thumbs and wondering what to do next. So it's always a good idea to have an alternate plan.

After you formulate your plans, put your information in a carrying case or bag. Include maps, addresses, phone numbers, etc., for all the places you'll be going and any alternate places you might like to consider.

To get the most out of your trail riding adventures, choose your traveling and riding buddies carefully. These people are enjoying an afternoon break on a mountain top in Colorado.

Maps to Go

After obtaining information, the fun begins with deciding where to go. Pick areas that have several trailheads and a good safe camping area. Usually included in the tourist or recreational information packet that you'll receive is a description of the area and an overview map or printed descriptions of the trails and the rules governing your stay.

There's usually a form included with which, for a small fee, you can order a more detailed topographic map. For areas that you know you definitely want to ride, order the map so you can be somewhat familiar with the trails. But, if you're not sure, you can always stop at the forest service or park office and pick up a map.

Traveling Partners

Probably one of the most overlooked factors affecting the success of any trip is the people with whom you'll be traveling. Consider them very carefully. If you're planning an adventure with your spouse, your family or a friend, make sure your traveling partner is someone you get along with. Close quarters and quick decisions are more manageable if you get along with one another.

The learning curve can be made a little easier by taking weekend trips for a while and then slowly adding days to your trip to help elevate the stress. This gives you time to learn how to maneuver around each other in tight spaces, figure out schedules for your everyday routine and how best to have fun together.

Another way to help make your trip go smoothly is to work together with your partner. It's much easier to have jobs you're responsible for, and that way everything should get done. Divide the duties according to your expertise, if possible. One can do the planning and keep the camper ready to go. The other can be responsible for taking care of the maintenance on the truck, trailer and so forth. If children are involved, give them age-appropriate responsibilities also.

A lot of things can go awry on the road. It's very helpful and perhaps imperative that each person understands how to do the other person's jobs. Learn how to work equipment, hook up the trailer, change a tire, drive the rig – everything in case you have to use it.

It's also important, if you're traveling with other rigs, that all people involved are compatible. We all have our own way of doing things,

Wearing orange vests during hunting season helps keep you from becoming the "target."

and, if there's someone who disrupts the group at home, they'll surely do it on a trip. So a word to the wise is to travel with folks you're comfortable with.

The more people you travel with, the more problems that might arise. If six couples take a trip together, that equates to six rigs with at least 48 tires that can go flat, 12 people and a dozen ways of doing things, at least 12 horses with 48 shod feet. So far we're up to 126 potential problems and the list goes on and on. Get the picture? There's nothing wrong with leaving at the same time, traveling at your own speed, then meeting everyone at an agreed-upon spot in the evening.

More Tips for the Road Warrior

Keep in mind the season in which you're traveling. Traveling during the "off" season makes life much simpler. Facilities are far less crowded than at the height of the tourist season. Although that's not always possible, for most people it's something to consider.

Find out if it's hunting season in the area you're planning to visit. If it is, be cautious and wear an orange vest and other bright attire while riding, so you won't be confused as the "target." Don your horse's neck, legs and tail with strips of hunter's orange, as well, so he's not mistaken for an elk or deer.

Another thing to consider on your road trip is navigating through large cities, especially at rush hour. It's always best to leave early in the morning, have a long lunch, or otherwise arrange your schedule so you avoid the rush-hour traffic.

Also, while you're on the road, there's always the need to stop to replenish your water supply and to dump your black and gray water tanks. This can usually be accomplished at places like large truck stops, city parks, state parks and fairgrounds. Other possibilities include private campgrounds (for a fee) and on some interstate highway rest areas.

The Voice of Experience

Once you've learned all about your destination, where you can and cannot ride, and you've made all the plans possible, realize that there's always something that manages to change them. However, that isn't necessarily a bad thing. As your learning curve continues to grow and your knowledge of traveling grows, you'll be able to travel about the country without any problems.

The best overall advice for the traveling trail rider is to keep things simple. When things begin to get complicated, it can take the fun and interest right out of it. The less complicated life is on the road, the more likely it is to go smoothly. Don't try to do it all on one trip. Don't try to have all the fancy equipment that you didn't have time to learn how to use before you left. A little motto for the road: Don't give up, don't get mad, just do something different.

11 CAMPING AND HORSE FACILITIES

Camping with your horse has to be one of the most rewarding experiences for the dyed-in-the-wool adventure trail rider. This developed camp site in the White River National Forest near Meeker, Colorado, is one of Janine's favorites.

It's common when starting out on your trail riding excursions to not know what overnight and camping facilities are available to you as a horseman. It's not easy to sort out this information in your own area, let alone in a different state or across the country. There are campgrounds and horse facilities all over the country and with new ones springing up all the time, there are literally thousands of good camping sites and overnight services for the horseman. Your choices vary from the deluxe bed, breakfast, and barn to a dispersed backcountry camping area for the quiet get-away experience and everything in between.

Private Facilities

Many private establishments, specifically bed, breakfast and barns, are beautiful, first-class equine resorts. A "five-star" facility might offer suites, gourmet meals, massages and hot tubs. However, the majority of private businesses include stables, horse motel/hotels, regular hotels with corrals (located mainly in the West near resort towns) and private campgrounds with and without corrals. Amenities can include electric and water hook-ups for your rig and facilities for your horses' comfort. They might even have a small general/grocery store, laundry, game room and much more. Some have arenas and round pens and are near trails for your riding pleasure. The fees for these facilities vary greatly and you generally need reservations.

Government Facilities

State, local and national agencies also offer camping facilities but they're usually much more conservative in nature. The following are some terms that might help you understand what's available at these places.

Full-service campgrounds:

A full-service campground has most everything you need, such as electric and water hook-ups at each individual site, corrals/stalls and showers/bath houses. Many have other amenities to make your stay as comfortable as possible. They're usually very popular and require reservations.

Developed campgrounds:

A developed campground has individual sites, but if electricity is available they could be located where several units can use the same outlet. Water for humans and/or horses might also be distributed throughout the camp. Developed horse camps generally have corrals, highlines, hitching posts, toilets and showers (nearby) for your convenience.

Primitive horse campgrounds:

These national forest and BLM campgrounds don't offer individual sites and the amenities are sparse, including available water. However, there might be corrals or highlines and centrally located toilets.

Dispersed camping:

Dispersed camping means primitive sites, which offer very little if anything as far as amenities. They're simply "pull off the road"

The Inn at Rockhouse, near Gunnison, Colorado, is a bed, breakfast and barn with fantastic amenities, staff and trails.

The stalls at many private facilities, as well as at most state fairgrounds, are safe and comfortable.

Sturdy corrals in national forests are a welcome site to weary traveling trail riders. These are at Hoop Lake in northeastern Utah.

Camping at the trailhead, such as this one in Washington State's Olympic National Forest, is always a possibility for the trail rider.

Fairgrounds are great places for an overnight stay on your way to trailheads.

places with no facilities. The preferred spots for horse people are alongside a stream or other water source for your stock.

Trailhead parking:

Trailhead parking spots generally allow overnight camping unless otherwise posted. They generally have no facilities, other than the occasional outhouse.

Non-horse campgrounds:

Run by the national forest or the BLM, they are developed campgrounds that generally don't allow horses within their boundaries. However, you can certainly camp in the sites yourself and find a place near the camp to highline, picket or confine your horse in some way.

Other Facilities

Fairgrounds and rodeo grounds are popular for the overnight stay. You have a safe place for your horse and many fairgrounds have camping facilities, complete with full hook-ups. Stockyards might be a place you can overnight your horse, while you park your camper in the parking lot or stay at a private campground. Some veterinarian offices have stalls or pens they rent out for an overnight stay.

Power Supply

If you camp in an area where facilities are limited, there are a couple of alternatives you might want to consider for your power supply. A portable generator or one that can be installed in or on your camper or trailer can provide the needed electricity for most of your needs.

Another possibility is solar panels, which are more than adequate to keep the batteries in your camper charged, although they won't run your microwave or air conditioning. Solar panels can be installed on the roof of your living area, or you might choose to have a portable panel that you can place in the direction of the sun when you arrive at your destination.

Portable or Electric Corrals

Bringing along your own form of horse confinement is a necessity for the traveling trail rider. There are several ways to keep your horses safe and sound at your camp. Choices are strictly a matter of personal preference, for the most part.

Electric fencing is a quick and easy way to contain your horse. It's simply a matter of placing some poles in the ground, stringing the electric tape through the poles, applying a power source and enclosing the horse. Make sure you familiarize your horse with this form of confinement prior to your trip; otherwise, he might not know what the thin, barely visible tape is all about, become confused and run right through it. The electric shock would scare him and cause him to run off in fear. Now you're at your camp, but the horse left for home.

Electric fence kits are available from many sources and are ready to go. On the other hand, you can put together your own kit with items to be found at your local feed or farm supply store. They usually carry a variety of poles, electric tape and fence chargers. With a little ingenuity, your fence can be your own creation.

Portable corral panels are another handy way to make a home-away-from-home for your horse in a hurry. You can carry them inside your trailer or attached to the outside with pins, bolts or clamps. However, purchase the lightweight variety, so you won't add extra weight to your trailer. If you use the panels to contain your horse, make sure they're secure enough so they don't fall over if your horse leans against them.

Rope Confinement

Highlines are popular for overnight camping with horses. They're usually made of ½- inch or

Horses should respect electric fencing before you use it in the backcountry.

You can make your own electric fence with poles and electric tape.

These two buddies are stationed near one another but on separate highlines. Note the height of the highline and the tree-savers. Also, the lead ropes are long enough to allow the horses to hold their heads naturally and even graze.

Pickets give the horse limited freedom, but are good restraints when no corrals are in sight.

Picket pins should have wide flat tops for pounding them into the ground and swivels so the picket rope can turn 360 degrees.

larger diameter, non-stretchable rope about 40 feet long. Nylon, poly or yachting rope are good choices as they weather well. Tie the rope between two trees high enough so a horse can get his head under it. Always use tree-savers placed around the tree so the rope won't score the trunk. You can purchase them from an outfitter's supply store or make them yourself from heavy canvas straps or old inner tubes. If you have more than one horse on a highline, use rings or knots spaced along the rope to help keep the horses from becoming tangled up with one another.

Tie your horse to the highline with a lead rope that's not so short he can't hold his head at a normal level. The length should allow your horse to lower his head to the ground for eating hay or grazing, but not be so long that he can get his leg over it.

LIFE ON THE TRAIL

Barely Visible

The Great Smoky Mountains National Park, one of the most beautiful places in the country to ride and camp with your horse, is known for its many black bears. Jim and I were riding down a trail filled with huge old-growth trees, breathtaking rhododendron and gorgeous mountain laurel when we spotted a lone hiker coming toward us. I couldn't help but notice that there was something different about the hiker, and Jim was equally puzzled. Suddenly, we saw the hiker stop, take something out of his fanny pack and pull it over his shoes and up to his waist. We then realized he was putting on his shorts. He'd been hiking in the nude! As the man approached us, he asked us where a certain resort was. I had to turn my head to keep from laughing at the thought of this older man naked. After he passed us, I mentioned to Jim that that man had put a whole new twist on the concept of bears in the Smokies.

The picketing method uses a one-leg hobble and long rope attached to a picket pin. It's definitely not for every horse; however, there are people who use it all the time and are very happy with this system. A picket usually includes a solid steel picket pin with a durable swivel that allows the horse to move 360 degrees around the pin. The pin should be wide at the top, which makes it easier to pound into the ground.

The system generally includes a soft cotton rope, about 30 feet long, and a one-leg hobble, made of neoprene, leather or nylon. After attaching the hobble, always walk your horse to the end of the rope so that he'll know where his parameters are. Your horse should be used to this method before you try it for the first time out on the trail.

Two-leg hobbles are generally made of soft nylon rope or leather. They attach around a horse's front legs, yet still allow the animal limited movement. Putting a horse's front legs in hobbles is good for daylight hours, but don't leave them on overnight. He could manage to hurt himself and even hobbled, can travel long distances. Backcountry outfitters often use hobbles to control their stock, but then the animals are used to this form of confinement on a daily basis. Your horse more than likely isn't, so be cautious in trapping his feet when you can't be there to get him out of trouble.

Like highlines, you can buy pickets and hobbles from any outfitter supply store, and some tack and feed stores carry them, as well.

A word of caution: No matter what form of confinement you choose, there are risks. If there's a way to get hurt, a horse can find it with any piece of equipment.

Weed-Free Hay

Certified weed-free hay might be required for some national forest and BLM lands, so check with the district office prior to your arrival date. Such forage is grown by farmers and ranchers who comply with certain state rules and regulations regarding their hay fields. You can find their names and phone numbers by calling the state department of agriculture. The thinking behind weed-free hay is that forests can be infested with weed seeds brought in through horse manure. To prevent a forest from becoming overgrown with weeds, thus killing the native plants, it's necessary to enforce rules that ensure trail horses and other livestock are free of weed seeds for a certain time period, usually at least 48 hours, before coming to the area. If you know you're going to ride in an area that requires weed-free hay, you should feed your horses certified hay for a few days before the trip. Government officials might allow you to use pelleted feed instead of weed-free hay, which is sometimes easier to obtain. You can also get a list of places where hay or feed can be purchased in the area, so be sure to ask.

Good Questions to Ask

Other questions to ask before you arrive are some I've mentioned before but they're so important they bear repeating. Is water available for you and your horse at the campground and on the trail? What are the regulations for the camp and trails? What are the conditions of the roads and trails?

LIFE ON THE TRAIL

Poof, it's Gone!

One time while traveling a long day, in bad weather, we couldn't wait to get to our destination - a city-run stable where we'd stayed several times. In fact we'd just been there a couple of months earlier. As we approached the street where we turned to enter the stables, things looked drastically different, although it was dark. On closer inspection, we could see that the stable was no longer there. It'd turned into an open field. What a shock! Now what would we do? Jim noticed a man in a cowboy hat at the service station next to us. The man told him of a stable that would take us for the night. He also explained that the city stable had been torn down to make way for a new department store. You never know what might happen, so expect the unexpected.

Ask about wild animals in the area, especially if any bears are known to frequent the campgrounds. Take appropriate action to keep food and garbage from around your campsite. Make sure your food is kept inside your camper or trailer or contained in bear-proof containers. Sometimes this isn't good enough as bears have been known to break into tents and even campers and trash the place in search of food. Bears can be very destructive!

The Unexpected

When camping with horses, be prepared for the unexpected. Sometimes, things aren't what they were touted to be or as safe as you'd hoped they'd be. Unfortunately, that is just a part of life, and you have to learn to deal with it and move on. However, don't be afraid to voice your displeasure to the proper authorities, in the form of a phone call, written complaint or in person.

12 MOUNTAIN RIDING

One of the best ways to experience the grandeur of the mountains is on the back of a horse.

Towering peaks, wild-flower meadows, spectacular vistas and quiet solitude are just a few of the lures of the mountains for many trail riders. Mountain riding might be your goal, but your dreams can easily turn to nightmares if you don't prepare yourself and your horse for the challenges.

Both the Eastern and Western mountains are adorned with beautiful wild flowers dotted among the lush green meadows, surrounded by majestic oak and pine forests, but the similarities end there.

The Eastern mountains are much older than those of the West, and, consequently, through erosion over time, their slopes are more gentle, making the elevation changes tolerable for horse and rider. However, they're densely forested and have thick underbrush, which makes cross-country travel difficult.

The Western mountains are steeper than their Eastern counterparts, as a result of more recent volcanic activity. The terrain is extremely rugged, but the Ponderosa pine forests can allow the rider to venture off trail in certain areas. However, high altitudes are a challenge not to be taken lightly.

The Riding Season

The best seasons to ride in the mountains vary all over the country. With a little research into the climate and geography of an area, you can pick and choose your destination knowing fairly well what to expect based on the usual scenarios for a particular area.

The mountain riding season in the Eastern and Midwestern half of the country begins in spring, but you might have to face some obstacles. The snow usually melts off in the early spring, around the end of March or the first of April, making mud one of your horse's enemies. The mud or muck can suck your horse's shoes off, cause leg injuries and might even be deep enough to get your horse stuck.

Spring temperatures bring out the mosquitoes, ticks, flies and gnats. The copperheads, rattlesnakes and other venomous snakes crawl out of their dens during the warm months. Later in the season, from late June to early September, the huge horse flies and the deer flies can be a real menace to your horse. Coupled with the high temperatures and humidity, life on the trail can be pretty miserable for you and your horse. Even the mountains give little relief to human or beast, so stock up on fly spray for both.

Fall is generally a beautiful time of the year to ride in the Eastern half of the county, but winter with its snow, cold weather and high humidity is one in which very few folks, if any, venture out to ride their horses. Chilled to the bone is an expression most Easterners and

Springtime in the Rockies can still mean snow in the high country.

Midwesterners use to characterize themselves in their winters.

In the West, you've a much smaller window of opportunity for trail riding. Typically the snow doesn't melt off the high-country trails until late June or early July. However, it's not unusual to have snow linger in some mountain ranges for most of the summer. It might be fun to ride through small patches where the surrounding area is exposed and you have a pretty good idea there's nothing under the snow that could cause your horse problems. On the other hand, it wouldn't be a good idea to ride through a patch of snow located in the middle of a forest of blown-downed trees, or a really rocky area. Don't take chances. You could be miles away from trailhead and hundreds of miles from the nearest hospital or veterinarian.

There are even areas in the Rockies when snow remains on the trails all year. There's also the possibility snow can fall as early as August, although it usually doesn't occur until September in the higher elevations. Call the ranger's office and check on the conditions in the area you're planning to ride.

The Western mountains, with elevations that can reach over 14,000 feet, can be a real summer get-away for the horseman who wants to escape the heat of the flatlands. Along with the nice cool days, however, the temperatures can dip into the thirties or colder at night, so you'll want to be prepared with a winter coat for you and blankets for your horse.

The low humidity of the West can make the sunshine feel very good to you on a chilly morning. However, the long-sleeved shirts you see the local people wearing aren't only for the chill; they also protect their arms from the

Walk over patches of snow carefully. You don't know what's underneath it.

LIFE ON THE TRAIL

In a Fog

One of the most frightening riding experiences we've ever had was in the mountains of Virginia when a thick fog rolled in while we were riding in a new area. I literally couldn't see my hands on the reins, let alone the folks we were riding with. We decided that it would be safer to stop and wait for the fog to clear than to try to ride in the thick soup.

As we waited for the fog to lift, we could actually hear other riders and hikers talking around us, but we had no idea where they were. What a strange experience.

intense rays of the sun. Wide-brimmed cowboy hats aren't worn just for looks – they help shade faces and necks. It's important to protect your skin in the higher elevations no matter what the temperature is.

Another advantage of the higher elevations of the Western mountains is the seemingly smaller population of pesky insects. Make no mistake, they're still there, along with ticks and horse and deer flies, but they don't seem as ravenous as their Eastern cousins. A rare site in elevations over 8,000 feet is the venomous snake – it's just too cold for slithery creatures.

The Spring Thaw

While riding in the mountains in any part of the country during springtime, pay attention to conditions caused by the spring thaw. When the snow melts, the water has to go some-where. It generally runs into creeks and rivers, causing them to rise quickly, making crossings extremely dangerous. Swift and swollen water might not be something you should attempt to cross, even under the best circumstances.

Gentle streams, like this one, can become raging rivers after the spring thaw.

Rain, Thunder and Lightning

The monsoon season can be a time of the year that's not conducive to trail riding in the mountainous areas of the West. Drenching rains and driving winds, coming from the south and southwest off the Pacific Ocean, can be a deal breaker for your long-planned horse vacation. No one really likes to ride all day in the rain, especially a soaking rain in the cool mountains. Sloshing through a wet forest and mud, then having to go back to camp and clean tack is not a fun way to spend the day.

Thunderstorms are common in any mountain range, but especially in the West because of the giant clashes of hot and cold air prevalent in that part of the country. You'd be well-advised to schedule your day's trip around them if possible by starting out early in the morning, as most thunderstorms occur in the afternoon. Head down to a lower elevation before the storm hits.

In addition to the rain, lightening or hail, there are also the dangers of slippery footing and falling tree limbs.

If you should be at the top of a peak or in an open meadow when a storm strikes, seek shelter as soon as possible. Although we've been taught to stay out of trees, it's far safer to be in them than in an open field. If you're caught in the open with nowhere to go, get off your horse and let him go. His metal shoes might attract lightning, and you don't want to be anywhere near him at that point. Get as low to the ground as possible, curling up in a ball, which makes you a smaller target. Don't remain close to your riding partner either; spread out. If one person is hit by lightening and you are close, lightening can actually jump to you. Therefore, give yourself and others plenty of room.

Wet conditions might also make driving difficult. If your adventure has taken you off the beaten path, you might want to consider the road type. Dirt, sand and clay roads can become extremely slippery and impassable when wet. Again use your common sense. Check the weather forecast and think about what it can do to the road you'll be traveling. There's always another day or a different place to ride and camp.

Boggy Mess

Bogs are caused by wet conditions, generally in low-lying areas. They pose a real danger because they're often hard to see, and

Ride carefully through wet, potentially boggy areas. This horse closely watches where he puts his feet.

you can easily find yourself in the middle of one if you aren't paying attention. Bogs in the Western states are usually harder to detect than bogs in the Eastern states. Marshes in the East are mostly around ponds, lakes and rivers. Western bogs can be found in a variety of places in addition to the normal bodies of water, such as areas of recent large snow melt.

Most experienced trail horses won't enter a bog by their own volition. The savvy trail horse knows his way around this hazard. However, if you and your horse are inexperienced, you might find yourself in the middle of a bog with your horse up to his belly in muck. The first thing to do is stay calm. It's best to stay on your horse if you can. He'll have to lunge to get out of the mess, and you wouldn't want to be in his way. Stay as balanced in the saddle as you can so you don't interfere with his ability to free himself.

Hunting and Horsemen Don't Mix

Camping and riding during the fall of the year has its obvious drawbacks because of hunting season. Before you venture out into the woods, check on the hunting schedules through the Department of Natural Resources in the state you'll be visiting. Seasons vary all over the country and can begin as early as August, such as archery season in Colorado, and extend as late as January in Florida. This is prime riding time for many trail riders, so be cognizant of sharing the woods with armed and dangerous hunters.

Archery and black powder seasons are the first allowed, but they generally involve a smaller percentage of hunters and, therefore, a shorter time period.

Never leave camp without preparing for inclement weather. Carry a coat and rain slicker with you at all times.

93

LIFE ON THE TRAIL

Gasping for Air

I had my wake-up call regarding the effects of high altitude on one of our first trips to the high country of Colorado. We'd just started out on the trail, at about 9,000 feet, when a thunderstorm suddenly erupted. The hail was so bad that my horse stopped and turned his hindquarters to the wind. This was his way of telling me that he wasn't going any farther. Things weren't pleasant for me either, as the hail pelted my face, hands and chest. The sting was horrible.

I had a new saddle, so I took the time to strip it off my horse, turn it upside down and lay it beside the trail, knowing that I couldn't carry it back to camp. It took all of my energy to just take it off my horse.

As Max stood there, butt to the wind, I decided to get back to camp and get out of the battering hailstones. My whole body was stinging from the hail, and all I wanted to do was get out of the chaos. I started running back to camp. Back East I ran several miles a day routinely, but within a few steps I was totally out of breath. By the time I walked back to camp, which was about a quarter of a mile, I was absolutely worn out and gasping for air. As I was trying to recover, the storm subsided. I looked out into the clearing sky and spotted Max heading back at a full gallop. He didn't seem to be as affected by the elevation as I was.

These riders stop for a break while climbing the Abajo Mountains in Utah.

The Rocky Mountains are majestic, but beware the dangers of rapidly changing weather conditions and high altitude sickness.

Riders traverse slowly over this rocky Wyoming trail.

Gun and rifle season brings out the most hunters across the country. A shot that doesn't hit its target can travel for miles and possibly hit you or your horse, which makes this season by far the most dangerous. Arrows and the ammo from black powder rifles have limited range, unlike bullets.

The most populated day of the hunt is the first day. You might be wise to skip riding that day. However, whenever you ride, whether the first or the last day of hunting season, make sure you and your horse are visible to all that might be in the woods, especially if that person has a gun. Keep in mind that hunters might be camouflaged so they're harder to see.

Never go riding during hunting season without a bright orange vest, hat, gloves and anything else you can wear that is brightly colored. Decorate your horse with all the bright orange you can find. Orange surveyors tape is a handy item to hang from your horse's mane, tail, bridle and saddle.

Rocky Mountain High

The high elevations of the mountainous West are a definite concern for riders from lower altitudes. Altitude sickness, which often occurs over 8,000 feet, is one of the

LIFE ON THE TRAIL

Cliff hanger

There are times when no matter how experienced you are on the trail, you might become a little unnerved. Such was my case when I encountered the cliff-edge trail in the Lizard Head Wilderness of the Colorado Rockies. The first time I rode it, I was scared to death. The edge – at over 12,000 feet in elevation - was about a mile long with a drop-off of 1,500 to 2,000 feet. There's absolutely no way to escape the path as the whole cliff surface is rock-covered. I wasn't the only one in our group feeling the altitude. However, we all made it across without incident and have returned to ride it several times since.

Unfortunately, one time there was a hiker who didn't have the support of her husband as he went hiking along his merry way while she was on her hands and knees crawling back to the safety of the tree line. She made it and her relief was evident. I would've offered her my horse, but she obviously wasn't going to give up the security of good ol' Mother Earth.

LIFE ON THE TRAIL

If a Tree Falls in the Forest

Once while riding in the Flat Top Wilderness of Colorado, a group of us had stopped to give our horses a drink from a crystal-clear mountain stream in a grove of aspen. As the six of us lined one side of the stream letting our horses enjoyed their break, what sounded like a shotgun blast rang out and a large aspen fell within a few feet of us. It took a few minutes to calm the horses and let our hearts settle back down from our throats. You just never can tell what might happen on the trail.

To keep from developing altitude sickness, don't start out your day with a lot of strenuous physical activity, which can bring on the symptoms. Take it slow and easy. If you start to experience any signs, stop exerting yourself in any way and get to a lower altitude. If they persist, seek medical help.

The best preparation for mountain riding and to help prevent altitude sickness is for you to be in good physical condition. Being fit at sea level, however, doesn't guarantee an easier time when you're over a mile high in the mountains. I've seen young people, long-distance runners and horsemen who've lived in the mountains all their lives have a tough time with high elevations. But if you're in good shape, your lungs might have an easier time coping with the thin mountain air.

Be careful with your equine friend in the high country, as well. A horse in top physical condition, such as the equine athletes that compete in competitive trail rides and endurance races, can handle higher elevations, but your flatland horse might not be as fit as you think he is. On steep and steady climbs, allow your horse to stop many times and catch his breath. A well-conditioned horse will do just fine if you give him a chance. Monitor his heart rate and respiration

most overlooked health concerns of the new mountain rider. The symptoms can be dizziness, fatigue, shortness of breath, nausea and/or headaches. Don't take this condition lightly. Some people have been known to die from it.

If you're planning to camp and ride in the mountains, give yourself a day or so in camp to acclimate. The air is thin up there, so expect to be short of breath most of the time. To fully acclimate takes much longer, weeks or months. Realize, though, that just because you're winded doesn't mean you've come down with altitude sickness. Other warning signs would have to appear for you to worry.

If you're in doubt about what lies ahead on the trail, tie your horse and check it out on foot.

as he goes. If he starts sweating profusely and breathing heavily, stop and take a break. If you'd like to see the altitude's effects, get off your horse and climb on your own two feet. That'll give you a new appreciation for what your horse is experiencing.

Climbing mountains in the West can be a real challenge. An ascent in the Rockies can go for miles, and the time it takes to reach the top is much longer than you're used to if you're from the East or Midwest. Even if you have a gaited horse, it would be a mistake to gait up a five-mile mountain trail before the horse has become acclimated.

On the Rocks

The Rocky Mountains, as well as most of the mountain ranges in the western U.S., didn't get their names from being a mound of sand or dirt. Rocky trails are extremely difficult for your horse to travel and they're hazardous. In addition to stumbling, he can injure his hoofs and legs, becoming very foot-sore and stone-bruised. He could even pull a tendon or ligament trying to dodge large boulders.

Make sure your horse is shod properly for this kind of terrain or wear hoof boots all around. Go slowly through the rocks and allow your horse to pick his way through. Don't try to rush him through a rugged area. Huge rocks on the trail might have to be stepped over, hopped up on and/or off of while maneuvering around trees. Many trails are covered with small jagged rocks or lava rock that can last for miles and are especially hard on horses' soles.

Get Off My Back

You might find yourself in a spot on a mountain trail where you're not sure if it's safe to continue. At that point, it's worth getting off your horse, tying him, then hiking up the trail to see whether it's safe enough to travel on or if you should look for a better route. Mountain trails can be tricky at times, and there's no sense in taking chances. A little hike up the trail to look around is much better in the long run than having to deal with trouble.

Unthinking Riders

One of the biggest problems encountered in the mountains is riders who give no consideration as to where they're riding. The fact is you simply can't ride in the mountains like you ride when you're at sea level. You can't gait or trot your horse through the miles of rocks, nor can you ride up miles of trails in high elevation without consequences.

You have to ride the mountains like they're mountains. It's that simple. Sadly, many riders don't heed the signs and their horses end up hurt and so do they. In addition to injuries to feet and legs, colic, tying up and even death can occur! Heed this warning: Use your head and slow down.

I've seen more than my share of horses brought from the Eastern and Midwestern states get hurt, or even worse. I have seen horses limp out of the wilderness. I've even ridden by a fresh corpse, and a few other times the bones of someone's equine friend. The images of these horses still haunt me. This isn't meant to discourage you from riding in the mountains. I don't want to instill fear in you about riding some of the most spectacular country you'll ever see. I want both you and your horse to have a safe, happy adventure. Think before and while you ride in the mountains and be safe.

LIFE ON THE TRAIL

A Mule's No Dummy

Once, while riding in the mountains out West, we rode with some friends from the Midwest. One of them had an endurance mule. Both were in great shape, and, in spite of warnings of the high altitude, they kept up their usual fast riding pace.

On the second day, as we were having lunch, her mule laid down. The lady thought her mule was suffering from colic. However, the mule wasn't showing the normal signs of colic or any other signs of illness. She seemed to have simply decided that she was just plain tired and wanted to rest. She refused to get up, and it took several people pulling on her lead rope to finally persuade her to stand. That wasn't the last time that she stopped to lie down at the higher elevations.

13 DESERT RIDING

The desert has a special beauty all its own. Janine's husband Jim and his horse Smoke ride in the Catalina State Park, outside Tucson, Arizona.

Trail riding in the desert and canyons of the West and Southwest can be an unbelievable experience. The sunrises and sunsets are some of the most spectacular anywhere and the scenery dramatic.

The popular desert riding seasons are during the fall, winter and spring. Summers, however, can be brutal with over 100-degree heat common for months.

The desert can be one of the most beautiful places to ride in the late spring when the cactus and the wildflowers are in bloom. Spring showers and snow-melt make the dry desert washes and streams come alive. In the fall of the year, colors of the trees and shrubs transform the desert into as beautiful a place to ride as you can find anywhere. Winters are sunny and notably mild with temperatures

The vistas of the Southwest canyon country are breathtaking.

Unlike other parts of the country, riding in the winter is always a possibility in the desert.

Being surrounded by astounding beauty won't matter if you run out of water.

LIFE ON THE TRAIL

that bring the "snowbirds" out of their dreary, cold northern climates.

But it's a Dry Heat!

That's what all the natives and transplants say about the desert air. It's hot, but it's dry. The desert Southwest has bragging rights about its 300-plus days of sunshine and a welcome lack of humidity, which makes high temperatures tolerable. With all the dryness, your skin might become itchy, so carry lotion with you. And along with all those sunny days comes ultraviolet rays, so don't forget plenty of sunscreen either.

Despite those concerns, blue skies and mild temps make for superb riding conditions. Snowbirds and retirees seek the Southwest for a good reason. Their riding season in the desert is much longer than other parts of the country.

There are a few weather- and terrain-related issues to contend with, however, so knowing typical desert hazards is a must.

Not a Drop to Drink

One of the perils you and your horse face is the lack of water. Other than in the spring, when the mountain snow melts and causes a runoff, or the occasional spring shower that leaves a few puddles, water isn't plentiful in the desert. There are a few natural springs here and there, but they're hard to find and might even dry up during the scorching summer heat.

No matter what the season, it's especially important for you and your horse to drink plenty of water in arid climates. One of the biggest dangers in desert riding is dehydration. You don't sweat like you do in humid climates; therefore, folks don't realize they could be in trouble. To avoid problems, carry plenty of water with you, and drink it. Don't wait until you think you've become thirsty. By that time you might be already dehydrated. Sipping water throughout your ride is the best way to keep sufficiently hydrated.

Also carry water in your rig for your horses. You can't count on finding water out on the trail. Even after a shower, puddles dry up quickly and desert springs can be few and far between. There are many portable water tanks on the market and some of them double as saddle racks.

A Prickly Place

Cacti, other succulent plants and water-sparing trees thrive in the dry heat and arid conditions of the desert and most all of them are prickly. They'll quickly grab your attention if you aren't careful. If you've ever been pricked by a cactus, then you know what I mean. Many species, especially the various kinds of cholla, have barbed tines that dig in deep and are hard to get out.

As they traverse through a desert, horses are vulnerable to the cacti and thorny trees. You'll undoubtedly have to remove a few cactus spines from your horse until he gets used to his new surroundings. He'll learn to steer clear of prickly plants in a hurry, but sometimes they're unavoidable.

To help remove the painful tines, carry a pair of tweezers, a multi-tool or a mane comb with you at all times. The latter is handy for

LIFE ON THE TRAIL

A puddle after a rainstorm might be all the water you get in the desert.

It's best to stay on established trails, rather than bushwack through the countryside. And even then, cactus can get a little too close for comfort.

plucking off buckhorn or jumping cholla pods that cling mercilessly to whomever gets anywhere near them. The pods (or buds) don't actually jump, but they seemingly have a way of reaching out to grab you as you ride by.

Be particularly careful when you encounter barrel cactus. Their fishhook-like spines can be extremely hazardous to your horse. In fact, we know of several cases of horses being put out of commission from their barrel cactus encounters.

Giant saguaro cacti are called the monarchs of the desert and are truly a sight to behold. Riding through them really makes you feel like you're in a Tom Mix western. These magnificent cacti exist only one place in the world and that's the Sonoran desert that stretches from the upper part of Mexico to just north of Phoenix, Arizona. The best place to appreciate them is from a distance, however. You don't want to accidentally rub up close to them horseback. Wearing thick leather chaps or chinks are an additional layer of leg protection against the desert's thorny defenses.

When you're through with your ride, remember to check for stickers on your horse's legs by running your hand up and down them. However, this is certainly not to say that you'll bump into cactus every trip. On the contrary, the vast majority of desert rides, and certainly those where you stay on established trails, are problem-free.

A Grain of Sand

Sandy washes or arroyos are great to ride in. It's fun to trot, gait or lope through them, but they should be ridden with care. Plowing through deep sand is a lot of work for your horse. True, it's soft, but because there's no "bottom" to it, it's very easy for an unconditioned horse to injure his legs. The horse's hoofs sink into the sand because there's no solid, opposing force as there is with dirt or decomposed granite. Thus, sand has a "dead" feel to it, which places soft tissue, such as tendons, ligaments and muscles, under tremendous strain.

Riding through sandy washes won't hurt your horse for short distances, but don't go for miles (and some washes are that long) until you've given your horse's legs sufficient chance to toughen up to the terrain. That might take weeks, so if you're in the desert for a short trip, stay on established trails instead of exploring the washes. Out west, established trails are almost always on decomposed granite. There might be a little sand cover over them, but they're solid underneath.

It's also possible for a horse to become overheated if ridden for any distance. Horses have to pull through deep sand; they don't just skim the surface. Because of the exertion, their heart rates can be elevated just by walking.

Wet sandy washes or streambeds can contain quicksand - a real problem for your horse and extremely hard to get out of, if not impossible. The more he struggles, the deeper in he gets. The savvy trail horse tests these areas by first taking a step or two toward the sand. He'll then usually put his head down and smell the ground. At that point he'll either proceed through it or back up and look for another way to go. Trust your horse's instincts, take his advice and find another route.

LIFE ON THE TRAIL

Desert Dummies

While riding and camping on a beautiful mesa in Utah during the rainy season one year, we enjoyed the rare opportunity of seeing water running down the normally dry washes. It certainly was a sight to see. The fast and furious stream was gone in a few days, leaving behind the evidence of the massive power water has in rearranging the environment. The topography of the immediate area was forever changed although just as beautiful as before.

The last morning we spent in the area was clear and beautiful. We figured that after our day's ride the roads would be dry enough for us to get our rig out. As we were tacking up our horses, Max and Smoke seemed to be distracted and kept looking back toward the wash to our west. We rode in that direction to see what our horses were so curious about. There it was, a rig parked down in the wash! What in the world were these folks thinking? There was a large living quarters trailer and two horses tied to a tree, but the pickup that had towed the rig in was nowhere in sight. I couldn't believe anyone would camp in that spot. A few days earlier, the water in that wash was a raging torrent.

Later that day as we drove out to return home, we passed a truck coming into the area. It was a couple of hunters, no doubt novice desert riders, who'd come for deer season. Hope it didn't rain.

Flash floods can happen quickly in desert washes. Note the dark water "varnish" on the rock outcropping.

Preserving the beautiful moment on film is temping, but be mindful of ledges giving way in canyon country.

The desert is full of rocks, so much so, the ancients built their pit homes out of them.

Slick rock might be part of the trail, so take it slow and steady.

Flash Floods

The back roads, especially in the southwestern states, can become impassable when it rains or snows. Keep this in mind when you're traveling deep in the backcountry, otherwise you might spend an extra day or so because an unexpected rainstorm turned the road into a mucky slurry.

Canyon country can be extremely dangerous during a flash flood. This situation shouldn't be taken lightly, under any circumstances. Many people have been known to drown ignoring the signs. A small stream can turn into a torrent in a matter of minutes, and steep canyon walls are a death trap with rising flood waters. If you happen to get caught during a rainstorm, get out of the canyon as soon as possible or at least climb to higher ground.

Listen to weather forecasts to learn if heavy showers are predicted for the area or surrounding areas where you plan to camp and ride. Remember, flash flooding can be the result of a rainstorm miles from where you are.

Another potential danger of desert canyon country is the possibility of falling off the edge of the beautiful canyons. It's so tempting to get close to the cliff to try to get a better view of the unsurpassed beauty below you. Unfortunately, each year many people fall from ledges by stepping on a loose rock, slipping on a slick surface, having the cliff edge or rock give way or even by being blown off balance by a sudden gust of wind.

Rock Pile

The high deserts of the West, such as those in Colorado, New Mexico, Nevada and Utah, and the low deserts of the Southwest, such as the Sonoran Desert in Arizona, are extremely rocky, made up mostly of granite, sandstone and lava rock. Many established trails are just one big rock pile and negotiating through them can be extremely hard on your horse's hoofs and legs, not to mention your knees and shins should you bump into them. You'd be wise to have your horse shod or wear protec-

Big rocks and tight spaces can be a factor on desert rides.

tive hoof boots on all four feet to be prepared for these tough areas. And, just as they're good protection against thorny bushes and cactus, thick leather chaps or chinks might be your best friend in big boulder country.

Almost all the streambeds in the desert are composed of rocks. They're round and smooth from the action of water running over them for centuries, but that doesn't make them any less treacherous than their land cousins. Slick river rock is tricky for horses to walk over, especially when they can't see through the water to put their feet in safe places. Definitely allow your horse to pick his path slowly and carefully when crossing desert waterways.

Another kind of slick rock is weather-worn sandstone. There are many places in the desert West where you have to cross it just to continue on the established trail. Traction on your horse's feet and caution on your part are what you'll need.

Just as any place you ride in the country, the desert has its highs and lows and plusses and minuses, but, by far, its rewards outweigh its hazards.

14 RIDING ON OCEAN BEACHES

Long stretches of open beach – every trail rider's dream.

A favorite dream among trail riders is to gallop along a beautiful ocean beach with the waves splashing, the warmth of the sun on their faces and a cool ocean breeze flowing through their hair.

Reality, however, usually isn't quite like that, at least not right away. There are a few things to consider before your dream comes true. For example, finding public beaches where you can ride a horse takes a little research, and, when you get there, your horse might be scared to death of the "monster" ocean. Riding a freaked out horse takes all the fun out of a dream in a hurry. Your horse will also encounter things that he hasn't experienced before, such as the roar of the ocean, pounding waves and strange pieces of driftwood on shore, and he has no clue how to deal with them. Like any other new experience, go slowly and give your horse plenty of time to get used to his new surroundings.

On the Beach

There are places on both the East and West coasts and the Gulf Coast that allow horses on public beaches. However, there are far more opportunities on the Pacific Coast than on the Atlantic. Still, finding a public beach to ride on isn't as easy as riding in a national forest or regional park, where horses and trail riders are the norm. Beaches are the haven for swimmers, sunbathers, boaters and fisherman, who aren't used to seeing our four-legged friends, nor how to act arounding them.

Chances to have a beach to yourself increase after the tourist season, so check around and see what's available.

Beaches aren't trailheads, so parking your rig near them can become an issue, especially if the parking lots are designed for cars only and there isn't much room to maneuver a big rig. There are some public campgrounds near beaches, but you'll need to ask if they allow horses, most don't. This is especially true in areas that open their beaches to horses only after the busy tourist season or national park beaches, such as Cape Canaveral National Seashore in Florida.

Washington State offers a great place to ride from the town of Long Beach. You can stay at the fairgrounds, then ride a short distance through the small town to the beautiful beach, which boasts lots of riding.

There are several beaches in Oregon that are a horseman's paradise. The state park system has several places along its shores for horse camping and beach riding. The horse camps are primitive, but some have corrals and pit toilets. Despite the limited facilities, riding along the Pacific coast is worth it.

Just north of the town of North Bend is The Oregon Dunes National Recreation Area. Here you can camp in the White Mare Horse Camp while you ride the beach and the sand dunes.

California offers great riding opportunities at Port Reyes National Seashore, located north of San Francisco. You've a choice of riding the ocean beach or the high cliffs overlooking the ocean. However, you'll have to make arrangements to stay at a private facility in the area.

LIFE ON THE TRAIL

Beach Bum

Our first experience at an ocean beach was at Cape Canaveral National Seashore in Florida. We had to report to the office first. There we were told the rules, where we could park our rig and where we could enter the beach. We presented our current health papers and Coggins test and got our permit. We were then advised to place the permit where the ranger could see it and to be sure to take a shovel and a container with us to remove our horses' manure as we rode. It was really starting to wonder if this ride was going to be worth it.

Once we left the office we found the turnaround area and parked our rig on the street. After tacking up our horses we noticed the entry to the beach was a boardwalk. As we proceeded across the street from the boardwalk, we ran into dozens of people fishing and sightseeing. It became quite a feat to get through all the people. They seemed to be everywhere, waving their fishing rods over our horses' heads as we passed by.

To add to the confusion was the salty, fishy smell and roar of the ocean. And, of course, within just about a foot from the end of this boarded fiasco, Smoke decided to leave his first deposit of the day. Needless to say, all eyes were on Jim as he dismounted, got out his little shovel, scooped up and dumped the contents into the plastic bag I was holding.

Soon, however, we were able to enjoy the experience of riding along the ocean and traveled down the beach in hopes of getting a good view of the space shuttle launch pad.

Our horses were very curious about the waves, but, by this time, they were veteran trail horses and accustomed to the unusual. Still, we worked to make them comfortable with the new sights and sounds. As we did so, we hardly noticed a man lounging in a chair not far from us. When we rode by, he asked us if we saw the porpoises playing off in the distance. I turned toward him as he spoke, not wanting to be rude, then quickly turned back to the ocean view and rode off as quickly as I could. Jim caught up to me and confirmed what I thought I saw. The man was sunbathing in the nude! My embarrassment soon turned to laughter as we went on and got a glimpse of the shuttle actually in the launch pad.

Our return trip was much better as the nude sunbather was gone and most of the people on the boardwalk had also left. Although the trip started out a little on the tense side, it was worth the view of the shuttle.

After the tourist season, you can generally find ocean beaches all to yourself.

All sorts of strange stuff floats up on shore. These two riders and their horses check out a piece of barnacled driftwood.

Let your horse look at and smell the ocean before asking him to ride through it.

To find riding places on the beach, contact local riding clubs, state parks, national parks and recreational areas in the area in which you'd like to ride.

A New Monster

The first time you approach the ocean on horseback it's guaranteed to be an unforgettable experience for both you and your horse. There's absolutely no way you can prepare yourself or your horse beforehand for such an outing. It's definitely something that every adventurous horseman should experience at least once, in my opinion.

First things first. Forget about all the pictures and movies you've seen and the daydreams you've had about your beach excursion. It's extremely rare to take a horse that's never seen or experienced the ocean before, go down to the waves and start cantering up the beach as the horse calmly splashes through the water. That just won't happen in the majority of cases.

The smell of the salt water and the sound of the waves are the first things you and your horse will encounter. As you ride even closer, you'll be absolutely amazed at the vastness. You can't help but be taken aback the first time you see it. However, keep in mind that over the years you've seen a number of ocean pictures, watched it in on television and in movies, and you certainly know what to expect. You have a big advantage over your horse. Your equine partner hasn't had any prior knowledge of this "thing" in front of him. Be cognizant of the effect it's having on him. This isn't a little stream that he needs to cross; it isn't a lake you and he can swim in. It's a whole new ogre that he has to understand and deal with. In his mind, this monster could be the one that gets him.

As you approach the watery giant, pay attention to how your horse reacts. It's not hard to detect that ever fiber of his body will probably be working overtime. His first reaction might be to cut and run, so take a deep seat and be prepared to take a short hold of the reins for control, or dismount and lead your horse to the water if you feel more comfortable. At the very least, your horse might snort and come to a complete stop, eyes bugged out and ears targeted on the immense body of water, trying to comprehend it.

If he'll stand still and look, let him. Don't try to rush him toward the water's edge. That's the worst thing you can do with a frightened

Roaring, rushing waves are a whole new experience for the uninitiated beach horse.

If possible, ride with experienced beach horses for your horse's first time.

animal. He's trying his best to figure out what's in front of him, so give him the time to compute it in his brain. Relax and enjoy the view. If he seems braver after a few minutes, ask him to move closer to the ocean. He might take a few steps, then balk again. That's okay. Let him register that he got closer, and it didn't jump out at him. An approach-and-retreat technique is useful for teaching any new experience to your horse and is certainly an appropriate method for an ocean debut. Take a few steps forward, then move back, move forward again a few feet, then back. Repeat this pattern until you two have made it to the water's edge.

Don't get caught between the ocean and the rocks at high tide.

To be safe, ride in water no more than knee deep.

On the Water Front

Once there, just ask your horse to stand quietly as the waves come toward him. Let him get used to the sound and feel of the wave action on his feet and legs, but be prepared for his adverse reaction. He might try to head for higher ground again. Calm and reassure him by rubbing and talking to him, and he'll soon see that the waves, foam and noise aren't attacking him. Take the process slowly and let your horse, look, smell and take some steps to test his footing. If at all possible, ride with experienced beach horses that can help your horse learn the ropes.

After your horse has become accustomed to the whole situation, ride slowly alongside the water. The harder packed sand, nearest the water's edge, is easier for your horse to travel on. Wet sand is denser than dry sand. The farther away from the water, the deeper the sand and the harder it is on your horse. But the firmer footing is also closer to rushing waves and the foam, so be careful until your horse is used to it. If he hasn't been in deep sand before, take your time so he doesn't overexert himself. (See the section titled "A Grain of Sand" in the "Desert Riding" chapter for more information on the effects of deep sand on a horse.)

When his fear has been alleviated and his curiosity about the ocean and waves has been satisfied, your horse should visibly relax and start to enjoy the experience. Then it's safe to go faster than a walk. Start out by trotting and work your way up to a gallop. When your horse figures out how much fun it is, you'll get the ride of your life.

High Tide

Tidal action can affect your beach ride. The tide schedules are usually posted on bulletin boards in the area. If you don't see the schedule anywhere, ask someone in the know, such as the campground host or park official. The best time for a ride is as the tide is going out, or low tide. This gives you several hours to enjoy your ride on the beach.

Tide times are an important consideration, especially if the area is surrounded by steep cliffs or boulders that would make your exit a difficult one. You don't want to get trapped where you can't get out if the tide comes in. So, if you're in this kind of environment, don't go out for your ride until you check the tide schedule.

Another word of caution: Stick to the water's edge. Unless you're familiar with the ocean, its currents and drop-offs, you shouldn't venture out too far into the unknown. And, while it might be tempting, don't try to swim your horse in the ocean. The currents are too strong and could sweep you both away. Your horse might not be physically powerful enough to swim against them and won't understand why he should in the first place, so ride in water that's knee deep on your horse and no more.

15 ENCOUNTERS

Multiuse trails are the standard fare all over the country. It's the trail rider's responsibility to share them with other users.

I've noticed that there are far more users on the trail nowadays than when I started riding several years ago. It's a rare occasion to go out on a trail ride and not encounter another person, animal, bike, car or something else. Therefore, it's my contention that we, as trail riders, have the responsibility to make our ride as safe as possible and to represent our group (horsemen) as a courteous bunch.

Legs and Wheels

In most areas of the country you have to share the trails with other users, such as bicycles, ATVs, motorcycles and hikers. It's normal practice that these users give the right of way to the horseback rider. This is usually the case and these people are very courteous and accommodating to the horseman. The occasional cranky or non-thinking person is in the minority.

One negative aspect about mountain bikes is that they can be impossible to hear when they approach. A speeding cyclist can be upon you before you know it. Blind curves are especially dangerous. By the time you round the corner, it's too late and your horse doesn't have enough time to process that it's only a bike. He might become scared, and, at the very least, spook. At the worst, the cyclist could run into you or skid on his wheels trying to avoid a collision. So, use extra care when traveling on trails where bikes are a factor. You might even step off the path before coming to the curve in anticipation of a bike making the corner at the same time you do. If you can, ride during the week, as bike riders and hikers generally don't come out until the weekend.

Hikers are generally very friendly and nice to horse people. They step off the trail to let you by and often comment on the pretty horses. It's nice to say a few kind words and tell each other to have a nice day. However, there's a minority in the hiking community who seem to have an agenda, and it doesn't include horses on the trail. If you should encounter anyone who's unhappy about you and your horse being on the trail, it's best to just smile and move on. They're certainly not

LIFE ON THE TRAIL

Bumbling Bee-cylist

One beautiful afternoon in Cuyamaca Rancho State Park in southern California, we had an experience with a cyclist that I'll never forget. We were moving right along down the trail when our horses came to an abrupt halt. While I was settling back down into my saddle, I heard my friend say, "Wow, my horse thought you were a giant bumblebee!" I looked up and spotted a bicyclist, dressed totally in black cyclist clothing complete with bright yellow horizontal strips. His black-and-yellow striped helmet completed the bumblebee image. It took everything I could do to keep from laughing until he rode on by.

Two types of all-terrain-vehicles – horses and ATVs must find a way to get along in the backcountry.

LIFE ON THE TRAIL

Really Bugged

One winter we spent some time in the Ocala National Forest in Florida, camping and riding in the nice warm weather. One evening daughter Keely and I took Smoke and Max out for a little ride after supper in the beautiful forest of moss-covered live oaks, the kind you always see in pictures of the South.

After a couple of hours we decided we'd better head back to camp as it was beginning to get a little dark. As we neared the dirt road that would take us back, we could hear a real racket and a car horn honking. What a strange sound – honk, crash, honk, crash, honk, crash. Max and Smoke stopped and planted all four feet firmly on the ground, ready for a fast getaway, their eyes bugged out as they gazed at this "thing" coming down the road toward them.

As I tried to calm Max, I turned to see what the monster was. I couldn't believe my eyes but it was a Volkswagen "beetle" with its headlights flashing and horn blowing while its front end jerked up into the air and then came crashing down.

As this synchronized hopping machine came closer, our horses went to spinning and snorting out of fear. By this time, Keely had run out of patience and rode Smoke out into the middle of the road, waved her arms and yelled for the hopping monster to stop.

After a few more hops, honks and flashes, the couple saw us and stopped. They got out of the car and apologized for scaring our horses and politely said that they wouldn't start up again until we were safely down the road. Whew! I still wonder why this vehicle was so far out in the middle of nowhere! And why would they want a "bug" like that? I'll take a horse anytime!

LIFE ON THE TRAIL

Role Reversal

We'd been riding for years, dreading our inevitable encounter with horse-eating llamas. Finally, the day had arrived. We were riding in one of the most beautiful places in the country, Arch Canyon, Utah, near the small town of Blanding. As we rode closer to a couple of approaching hikers, we could see that the animals they were leading were not small horses, burros, goats or donkeys. They were llamas! My heart began to pound. A million thoughts were running through my head, mostly that my horse would go berserk the closer the "monsters" got to us. What to do, what to do.

Jim turned around and looked at me. The first thing I noticed was that he had no panic in his eyes. Why not? I'm sure he could clearly see panic in mine. My fear was alleviated a little when he said, "Janine, why don't we get off the horses and let the hikers go by us?" What a brilliant idea. Why didn't I think of that?

Jim and I dismounted and stood beside them, off the trail, as the hikers and their beasts of burden approached. The couple stopped to talk to us and were nice enough to point out some Anasazi ruins clinging to the sides of the spectacular red rock canyon. As we chatted with the hikers, I kept one eye on the llama next to me and my horse, Max. He seemed harmless enough. I noticed Max kept a close eye on the llama, too, although he didn't seem too concerned. I was just letting myself relax when suddenly Max gave one of his teeth-shattering shakes. Stirrups clanked, leather slapped and the llama jumped. Once the freaked-out llama was under control, I had to smile to myself. I realized my horse just spooked a llama! Perhaps it was sweet revenge for all the horses that had been scared to death by llamas.

A savvy trail horse can be your antenna and tell you when something is up ahead.

interested in your opinions on the subject anyway. There's no use in getting angry or exchanging words. It doesn't do anyone any good. Please keep in mind that you don't want to let anyone with a bad attitude spoil your beautiful ride.

Domesticated Animals

Domesticated animals, such as dogs, burros, llamas and even goats, are frequent on the trail. Dogs accompany many hikers as well as horseback riders. In fact, you'll be hard-pressed to find any riding group without a dog or two along for the ride. Therefore, most horses are used to dogs.

You trail dogs should behave and be under your control at all times. Make sure they don't bother other dogs, horses or hikers and the wildlife. As for burros, llamas and goats, your horse might be a little leery of them when encountered the first few times. In addition to looking different, they also smell strange to your horse and, therefore, give him pause, to say the least.

If your horse becomes upset over the sight or smell of these different trail users, the best thing to do is to try to ride around them, going far enough off the trail that you can avoid contact with them. If the circumstances make that impossible, then move to the side of the trail. Stay calm and try to keep your horse calm, as well. Rub his neck and talk to him. If possible, ask the hikers with the animals to stop so your horse can get a good look at them. Chances are the other animals will be just as curious about your horse. Once everyone calms down, pass the hikers and their animals slowly as they stand still or, if you're more comfortable, you stand with your horse until they pass by you.

Horses have been known to dump their riders and run away at the sight of something strange, like a llama. A veteran trail horse that's seen these long-necked monsters before might not pay any attention to the animal. If you're lucky enough to be riding with someone on an experienced horse with a "couldn't care less" attitude, ask that rider to lead and help your skittish horse get by the alien beings.

Backpack Monsters

The farther you travel into the backcountry, the fewer encounters you'll have with casual hikers and bikers. This is where you find the more serious outdoorsman, such as other adventurous trail riders, backpackers and commercial outfitters.

Many trail horses are accompanied by their owners' trail dogs.

If you're riding a green backcountry horse, backpackers might be a cause for alarm. At first sight, your horse might be convinced that this being with a huge pack reaching toward the sky is from outer space. However, if you get no response when you say hello to backpacker, ask him to speak in his usual voice so the horse will know that he's just a human being.

Wild Ones

You should never approach any wild animal, no matter the circumstances or what ideas you might have about them. Bears aren't teddy bears; buffalo aren't slow and lazy. Many people have been badly injured when they walked toward what seemed like a very docile animal only to be charged, trampled or run over by the wild beast. Don't try to get that one-in-a-million photo; don't try to show off for your mate and just simply don't take any chances.

Stop at the closest forest service office and ask if there have been any wild animal sightings in the area. You should also report any sightings you might have had yourself. This information can change your plans. I know that it certainly changed ours one time. When a ranger told us that a grizzly bear had attacked a hunter the day before in an area that we had planned to ride, we decided to find a trail that didn't have grizzly bears, like in another state. So off we went.

In addition to verifying wild animal activity with the forest service office, also check the bulletin board at the trailhead. Important and current information is usually posted there, and it'll help you become aware of what to expect on the trail.

Forest signs might be your first and only clue to the wildlife in the area.

Bear claw marks on the aspen tree tells you who was once there.

LIFE ON THE TRAIL

Who's Afraid of the Big Black Bear?

Although we've had countless encounters with black bears over the many years of trail riding, I'll never forget our first. It was a beautiful late spring day when we rode in Colorado's Weminuche Wilderness. As we followed the trail, which ran alongside the river swollen from the spring thaw, we passed a rickety old swinging bridge. The entrance to the bridge had been boarded shut, obviously because of the missing slats and poor condition. We continued on another mile or so until the trail disappeared into the swift and roaring river. In fact, the rushing water was so loud that Jim and I were unable to talk over the noise. With a high cliff to one side of us and the rushing water next to us, we had no choice but to turn around and go back to find another trail.

On the way back, I spotted a huge black bear on the other side of the river. I tried to let Jim know about the bear as it walked up onto the rickety old bridge and was making its way to our side of the river. With the bear sauntering across the bridge, we were on an intercept course. This wasn't a good feeling. I tried to make myself heard as I rode up next to Jim. Even at close range he couldn't make out what I was trying to tell him. By that time the huge, ambling bear was getting closer and closer. What to do?

I finally got Jim's attention by grabbing and shaking his arm as I pointed to the bear. As we came to a quick halt, I looked to the right, where I again saw the high cliff. To the left was the crashing, roaring river, and to the back of us, I knew, was a dead end. Our horses were intently focused on the bear, which was now about 75 feet from us. Too close, as far as I was concerned!

The wind was blowing in our direction, so he was unable to smell us. He'd not spotted us, and I knew that he couldn't possibly hear us. Out of nowhere I found, deep inside me, the most blood-curdling scream that I'd ever made in my life. I couldn't believe that it was coming from me. The bear stopped, stood up on his hind legs and looked right at us. I know for a fact that my heart had stopped! What was he going to do?

As the feeling of terror rushed through my body, the bear dropped to the ground and ran – in the opposite direction. We could see him crashing through the woods. I guess we looked a little too much for the bear to handle!

Know the Signs

If you're going to spend a lot of time in an area where wild animals are prevalent, educate yourself on their habits and the signs they leave behind. It's easy to buy a pocket guide to learn about their habitat, tracks and scat. As you ride, scan the trail and surrounding area for signs, such as paw prints or scratch marks in trees. Be on the alert, especially in designated wilderness areas where no motorized vehicles are allowed. Wild animals, especially large predator types, are shy and more prone to living in secluded areas than those with heavy traffic.

Wild animals are capable of killing or seriously injuring you and/or your horse. It doesn't matter what you've heard about predators such as bears and cougars not attacking people on horseback. That simply is NOT true. It doesn't happen very often, but it's something you should be aware of and take the appropriate precautions.

In all probability, you'll never encounter a bear or cougar on the trail. They'll hear or smell you and be gone long before you get close. Most are just as afraid of you as you are of them.

Wild animals are just that, wild. If you want a picture, you'll need to get it from afar.

Paw prints are probably all you'll ever see of the elusive cougar.

The size of the black bear is evident by the girl's size 10 shoes.

Avoid Them

One thing some trail riders have been known to do to help avert a wild animal encounter is to put sleigh bells on their horses, but actually that isn't very effective. The sound is simply not strong enough to carry far away. Think about it this way: Outfitters don't use sleigh bells when they turn their horses out for the night; they use cow bells. Cow bells, placed around the necks of lead mares or alpha geldings, make a pretty good sound and are used to not only ward off wild animals, but to tell the herd where the leader is and to give the outfitter a clue where to look for his stock. The only thing you accomplish with the sleigh bells is to irritate your fellow riders.

Talking loudly is a very effective way to scare off wildlife. How many times have you been riding with someone who has a loud voice, and you notice that you never see any wildlife when riding with that person?

Stings and Bites

Not all hazardous animals are predatory mammals. Bees, hornets and wasps can cause you and your horse untold misery. If you're allergic to bee stings, by all means, carry appropriate medication with on the trail.

Assume all bees are Africanized because, in many parts of the country, especially the South and Southwest, they are. Africanized bees are very aggressive and can attack with little provocation. Don't irritate bees by swatting at them, just steer clear and ride away.

Scorpions are a fact of life in many desert areas, so watch where you sit and where you place your hands. While they sting, rarely does

LIFE ON THE TRAIL

Busy Bees

The rain forest country of Washington State is absolutely beautiful, and we had the good fortune of riding there during the "dry" season, or at least it seemed that way at the time. However, our luck soon changed. We'd been on the trail for only a few minutes and were at the back of the line when some bees attacked Max. I thought it was a one-time incident and we all rode on.

Our ride continued for a few hours in some of the most beautiful old-growth forest I've ever seen. The trail meandered by huge ferns, moss-covered boulders and a beautiful flowing river. Suddenly, Max and now Smoke were hit with more stinging bees. The horses stomped and jumped as they tried to rid themselves of these terrible insects. That was it for me. I didn't want to run into any more so we decided to head back to camp. The other riders with us decided to return, even though they weren't getting stung.

On the way back, we were hit six more times. The other horses weren't being molested, which seemed odd. However, we didn't dare trade places in line with them. Jim and I just made the best of a bad situation.

We and our horses were burning with stings and my leg throbbed where it had been kicked in the fray. Eventually, we made it back to camp. What a battle! We spent the evening nursing our wounds and removing stingers from ourselves and our horses.

PHOTO BY JOHN BRASSEAUX

Poised to strike; heed his warning.

LIFE ON THE TRAIL

Rattle and Roll

Once we were riding in high weeds in the desert of Utah. Suddenly, we heard the rattle of the dreaded venomous Diamondback. What a scare to see this poisonous snake, coiled and ready to strike at Jim's horse, Smoke. It was even more amazing to see how fast a horse can spin and high-tail it out of there. I'm not sure whether Jim spun Smoke or Smoke spun on his own, I only know the four of us didn't stop running until we got to the trailer, where we loaded the horses and drove out of there faster than that snake had time to unwind.

it cause any long-lasting problems, although some people do have adverse reactions.

Rattlesnakes, water moccasins, copperheads and other venomous snakes, on the other hand, can be very serious for you and your horse. Few people die of snake bites, but there certainly are fatal cases every year. If bitten, remain calm, ride back to your rig and seek medical help immediately.

Being large animals, horses fair better with poisonous snake bites, which are usually on their legs, but the bites can still be nasty and need veterinary attention. However, a bite to the muzzle area is a red alert. A horse's nose

LIFE ON THE TRAIL

Gator-mate

Jim and I were riding near Doe Lake, in the Ocala National Forest of Florida. It was a gorgeous spring day and a beautiful trail ride. After a picnic lunch by the lake, we headed back to camp near Bass Lake. On our return trip Jim and I decided to put our horses in gait. We were riding at a fairly brisk pace when all of a sudden Jim's horse, Smoke, spun around in his tracks and headed straight back at me at full throttle. It was so unusual for him to do that.

Smoke stopped, turned back around and was staring at something very intently. Then I spotted it – a 20-foot alligator. (Well, that's how I remember it. Jim disagrees with my estimate.) Anyway, that alligator was up on all four legs running to beat the band. First it ran toward us, then with an abrupt turn it ran up an incline into the palmettos, stopped and turned toward us again. He didn't look all that friendly.

We took a wide sweep around the hill the ancient predator was on. We wanted to put as much room between us and the gator as possible, so we crashed through the palmetto brush trying to make our way back on to the trail and as far away as possible. As we maneuvered our way around the hill, none of us took our eyes off that gator. He sat on the hill and watched every move we made.

When we told our story to the local folks, they informed us it was alligator mating season. The male alligator had come out of his comfortable pond in search of a female friend. This explains why there weren't other people in the forest that time of year, except for us two swamp novices.

It took Smoke quite a while to get over the fact that logs don't move. He was convinced that downed logs could grow legs and come after him. I learned that the deep-throated frogs that croaked at night around the pond where we were camped were not frogs at all but male gators seeking company. You can be sure that we've not been back to Florida during gator mating season since then. We never will!

This alert horse thinks he sees a snake in the grass, but it's only a stick.

can swell shut in a hurry, thus cutting off your horse's breathing. Remember, horses can't breathe through their mouths. Carry a couple of small sections of garden hose, about six inches long, to place in your horse's nostrils if they start to close shut. That will at least give your horse an air supply until you can find help.

The trail, for all its rewards, still has its hazards in the form of humans and animals. Trail riding isn't for the faint of heart. You and your horse will have to be brave to face all sorts of encounters along the way. The saving grace is, the more you do it, the more experienced and braver you'll become and so will your horse. Exercising caution, being prepared and using good common sense are all part of responsible trail riding.

LIFE ON THE TRAIL

Bugged Out

One spring, while riding in the Ocala National Forest in Florida, Jim and I had a most unusual encounter. We'd been riding a couple of hours on sandy trails and through the beautiful live oak forests. During a break, I noticed a ladybug on my arm, then spotted another and another. I hadn't seen multiple ladybugs before and thought it interesting. About that time, my horse began swishing his tail at something, and I noticed Smoke doing the same. There were ladybugs everywhere. Not just a couple, but a couple hundred. We decided that it'd be a good idea to get out of there.

As we sped down the trail, we soon discovered that these red pests weren't flying away home, as the childhood rhyme says. They were increasing in numbers, and my horse was beginning to turn from grey to red. Soon, he was telling me very clearly that he wasn't happy. I saw that his face was totally covered with the bugs, including his eyes. I jumped off and began scooping the bugs from his eyes with both of my hands. I thought that I was in a Hitchcock movie. After several attempts, I could clearly see there were too many of these little invaders to conquer. Jim, who was having the same battle, said, "Let's try to ride out of them." I remounted and off we flew.

We didn't stop until we reached camp, where we found we were down to only a few hundred of the buggers. After a few hours, the majority had retreated. That evening and the following morning we could still find several ladybugs flying and crawling around in our motor home. In fact, it was literally months before we were totally free of the red spotted monsters.

16 GROUP RIDING

Group riding brings a whole new dimension to the trail experience. Your responsibility is not only to yourself, but to the others, as well.

When riding with a group, you and your horse enter a whole new world of riding and all the rules change, so to speak. You're no longer a lone trail rider with your focus on the relationship between you, your horse and your environment. You're now part of a group, and, as such, you have to be aware of you, your horse, your environment and the others in the group.

Group rides are all organized in some way, whether loosely by you and a couple of friends or formally by a riding club or a local organization. They're a great way to ride and socialize with like-minded people. They usually have relaxed rules, if any at all, allowing the participants to regulate the activities and their behavior themselves. The rides take place anywhere from an afternoon to several days and most of the rides involve lunch on the trail.

Commercially organized trail rides are more sophisticated in that they can handle hundreds of riders at one time. You pay a fee for the ride and for amenities, such electricity, water, stalls, a camping space, picket area, two or three prepared meals, shower house, entertainment and guided rides. The rules of the camp and its activities are spelled out very clearly to each patron so everyone has an understanding of what's expected of them.

The Down Side

Socializing and riding are the two main themes when riding with a trail group of any size. However, socializing might be limited to breaks on the trail and around camp. Surviving the ride itself might be your main concern because, along with all the positive things about group riding, there can also be negatives – some simply annoying, but some potentially dangerous. The more people and horses on the ride, the more problems present themselves. This is to be expected. Just prepare for it mentally, and you should come out of the event with good experiences and wonderful memories.

Here are some important points to keep in mind riding in any size group.

Follow the Leader

In any group, there's always a leader. One of the biggest responsibilities of the leader is the safety and control of the group. The pace of the ride is also determined by the first one in line. If the leader's horse walks on out, all the horses will have to walk fast to keep up; some will have to jog and some will end up jigging. It always seems that the horses at the end of the group have to move faster than those up front, in sort of a whip-like effect.

If you find yourself in the leader's position, realize that how you behave as trail boss affects the rest of the group. Make sure you know where all of the people behind you are, how they're doing, and, if need be, wait for them.

For example, when you stop at a stream to water your horse, realize that the rest of the group must have the chance to do the same. So, when your horse has finished and you've crossed to the other side, wait for the folks behind you to take their turn. Don't continue on down the trail, as the other horses will be more interested in keeping up with you than in drinking, or, if they stay to drink, then they'll want to run to catch up with you. The

Socializing with friends is one of the attractions of riding in groups.

The group leader has the responsibility for the ride's pace.

At a stream crossing, it's common trail courtesy to wait for the horse behind you to finish drinking before you leave.

best approach: After your horse finishes, simply move up to allow room for everyone. When all are through, move on down the trail.

Use this same technique for crossing any obstacle or at a place where horses have to slow down and take their time, such as through boggy areas and over downed trees. When you've maneuvered the obstacle, move forward and wait until everyone has gotten through the area safely.

If you don't want the liability for the tone of the ride that all leaders must assume, then don't ride in the front. Let someone else take that task and enjoy your ride somewhere else in the group.

Not Good for Green

Riding with a large group is best accomplished on the back of a well-broke, seasoned horse. If you or your horse is green, then start riding with smaller groups and trail savvy horses to give you and your horse the needed experience without the pressure to keep pace with the group.

If you accidentally find yourself in a larger group than anticipated, the best place to ride

Older, experienced horses are by far the best for group trail riding.

is as close to the front as possible, right behind the trail boss. Another option, is to find the calmest and most experienced horse and rider, then ride right behind them.

The same can be said for maneuvering a difficult obstacle or encountering a new situation that you're not sure how to navigate. In these situations you'd be wise to follow a more experienced horse. Most horses tend to do what the horse in front of them does. If that horse jumps, then the green one will want to jump. If the front horse is rattled, then he'll think there's something to be concerned about and become worked up as well.

If you feel the group is doing things or riding in places that you're not comfortable with and might be beyond your horse's abilities at this stage, then simply don't continue. Take another trail or return the way you came. Don't put your green horse and yourself in a situation that might have dire consequences. At the very least, he might pick up bad habits, such a jigging, from being nervous in the new situation. It's possible he could always associate big groups with a bad time, and you'll be limited to riding in small groups or alone.

A Word About Gaiting

Gaited horses, for the most part, are ridden "in gait" from the start of the ride to the end. Generally, as the rider sits down in the saddle and picks up the reins, his horse is off and gaiting. This, of course, is one of the reasons some trail riders buy a gaited horse. The "ride" itself is an experience that's comfortable and exciting.

This way of riding is perfect for easy trails with few or no obstacles. But, if you're on difficult trails with elevation changes, riding at high speeds becomes hazardous. The risks

Gaited horses can cover a lot of ground quickly. This group is gaiting their Fox Trotters across a mountain meadow.

increase even more in a group setting. In fact, the larger the group, the more dangerous it becomes.

If you're the first person in line, you have the advantage over the riders farther back. They have to control their horses at a high rate of speed, all the while trying to avoid obstacles. And, generally their horses become more excited. Under these circumstances it's a good idea to have a lead horse that, although gaited, can maintain a moderate speed rather than be the fastest of the group.

If you're a beginning rider on a gaited horse, you should avoid group riding, especially large groups, until you're in complete control of your horse, and, most importantly, you have the experience of riding on moderate to difficult trails.

When riding a gaited horse with non-gaited horses, be mindful that they probably won't move out as briskly or cover as much ground as you do. You might have to slow your pace to stay with the group.

Trail Etiquette

The important issue about trail etiquette is a matter of personal responsibility. Be cognizant of other trail riders in the group and have a sense of consideration for your fellow horsemen.

When you're in a group setting, there's usually a mixture of participants: experienced and novice riders, young and old riders and horses, gaited and non-gaited horses, slow and fast horses, considerate and inconsiderate people and a multitude of other opposites.

Unfortunately, there always seems to be at least one person in the group who just doesn't realize what a negative effect his activities have on other horses. Running his horse beside or up behind other horses puts those horses on the defensive and makes them upset and nervous.

It's okay to ask that person to slow down or not run up too close, etc. If you can, try to fix the problem before it becomes worse. However, some insensitive riders will just take offense and continue their inconsiderate ways. The best you can do at that point is steer clear of that rider and try to keep your horse from being affected by his.

The Nervous Wreck

It also seems that when one horse gets "out of sorts," it becomes contagious. Many a horseman has found his mild-mannered trail horse

LIFE ON THE TRAIL

Fine Finos

Although we don't attend many commercially organized trail rides now, we attended a number of them early in our trail riding days. One such ride was in the beautiful hills of Tennessee. During the weeklong ride we rode some breathtaking country, enjoyed the company of our dear friends Max and Gloria and made some new friends.

Frequently, we rode up front with the trail boss. He was a real story teller and many of his yarns were about some flatlanders who had attended the previous ride with Paso Fino horses. All week long we heard the stories of these little horses that had such a hard time in the hills of Tennessee. Fun was had by all at the expense of those poor flatland Pasos.

On the last day of the ride, while having lunch, the trail boss expressed what great trail horses Jim and I had. I'll never forget his exact words, "Those are two of the best trail horses I've ever seen. What are they, Arabs?" Jim and I looked at each other and then in unison said very proudly, "No, they're Paso Finos!" The look that came across his face was priceless, and we all broke out laughing.

suddenly turned into a real renegade. A horse that's completely out of control and driving you out of your mind is not the way you probably planned on spending a day of trail riding.

There are a few things that might be worth trying in this situation. First, move up to the front of the line and in back of the trail boss, or, if there is no trail boss, then have your horse take the lead. By putting your horse in a thinking mode, he might not have time to think of the antics going on behind him.

If you can't possibly make it to the front because the group is very large or the terrain doesn't allow you to change positions, find a calm horse close to you and ride behind it. Often, a quiet horse to follow is all you need to help your horse regain his cool.

If you know your horse is the one who could act up in a large group, try to avoid his poor behavior by longeing him beforehand. Letting off a little steam might get him in the right frame of mind for a crowded ride.

Who's on First?

In any herd of horses, even a newly formed trail group, horses know who the leader is or they try to figure it out. Following a leader is innate equine behavior. After millions of years of evolution, you can't change that. What you must do is understand it and work around it, especially when riding in a group.

During any breaks, don't tie strange horses next to one another, only stable mates.

In a trail riding situation, horses that are new to one another might fuss and fight until they determine who's the boss. Be careful not to ride too close to a strange horse until the two have become acquainted and made their peace.

Some horses just can't tolerate their space being invaded by a stranger. Always leave a horse's length between you and the horse in front of you, out of courtesy and for safety's sake.

What positions horses assume in a group line-up is also a consideration. Having two bickering horses ride next to each other isn't a good idea. Also, stable mates should probably stick together to avoid any separation anxiety. However, confident horses can ride anywhere in a group and behave.

Some horses can't stand not to be in front. They just won't ride well anywhere else. They jig, go sideways or just become a nervous wreck because they're not the leader. You have only two choices, well maybe three – always ride in front, train the horse to become less anxious or get another horse. The second

LIFE ON THE TRAIL

Circle of Influence

I used to circle my horse when he was younger, especially when going back to camp and horses were passing him as they hurried back. He figured if they could hurry back, why couldn't he? I never liked the idea of him racing back to camp, so I'd circle him until he got the message we weren't going to return at high speed. However, I didn't realize how much I was doing it until one day, as a horse sped by us on his way back to camp, before I thought about putting my horse in a circle, he started circling himself. Now that's a well-trained horse!

option is time-consuming and requires a savvy trail trainer – sometimes a professional trainer.

Some things to try are circling your horse or putting him to work by making him weave around trees, bushes or rocks. He might find that walking is more desirable than working. Another idea is to allow him to move to the front of the line, but push him 30 to 40 more feet up the trail, turn around and move back to your original place. When he seeks the front again, repeat the same procedure until he finds out that it's much more work to be in front than walk quietly in line.

The Return Trip

Returning to camp can turn into the worst part of the ride. If one person allows his horse to run back, the race is on. If you're in a group that takes turns taking the lead, then perhaps you might want to save your turn and use it when you need to calm your horse. That might very well be on the return trip.

It's not uncommon for horses to become hyper if they go back the same trail they went out on, or, if they're on a familiar trail, they realize the end of the ride is near. Many horses even know that after the lunch break, they're on their way back to camp.

Some horses quiet right down if allowed to lead. So, if the trail boss lets you and your horse needs to be in front, by all means be the leader. However, if your horse insists on hurrying back to camp, try circling him or the turn-back exercise mentioned above to help him regain his composure. The idea is to get his mind back to where it should be, on what you're telling him and not rushing back to camp.

Another possibility for calming your horse might be to put him in the back of the group. It's not unusual for some people to allow the faster horses to go on ahead, while others stay in the back and enjoy the scenery. Most of the time, you can only stay back if you have a horse that doesn't care about all the hoopla going on ahead of him. This might be a good place to ride your horse so he can see how others are handling this situation.

If your horse becomes out-of-control, simply leave the group. If he finds himself going in a different direction than the others, it'll give him something to think about, which is just what you need to gain back his attention and, therefore, control.

You might also want to stop and wait it out. If the others go on ahead, a break from the pack might be what you and your horse need. It's always best to do these things with another person.

Hide and Seek

There are times when you might stop to fix your tack or get distracted by something else and find the rest of your group has gotten out of your line of vision.

If you find yourself out of earshot of others, don't panic. An experienced trail horse might just be able to find the rest of the herd if you give him his head. Stay calm and let your horse walk back to the rest of the horses. Often, a lonely horse will whinny for the other horses, which helps locate the group.

Watch Your Shape

When having a great time with a group of friends, you might find yourself riding faster or longer than you're used to. Horses that aren't in the best shape, especially in the spring, can easily become overextended, and you might find your horse developing colic or tying up. Remember, horses aren't machines; you have to condition their bodies and legs for the sport. They're capable of much more than folks give them credit for; however, that's after they're conditioned and in shape for the rigors of an extensive ride. So, be kind to yourself and your horse, and take it easy until you both are in shape.

In a Perfect World

In a perfect world, it's best to ride with folks who have riding habits similar to yours, those who ride at the same pace and like to explore places you do. However, this isn't always possible. If you ride slower than the group, make an effort to not have them wait on you all the time, and, if you're the faster rider, slow down so your friends won't have to hurry up. Whatever the case might be, as a courteous trail rider, make the best of any situation.

To have a successful group ride, be considerate of all riders and recognize that people and horses have different personalities and skill levels. Don't do anything that could possibly put someone or his horse in danger. We're all out there to have fun and enjoy the great outdoors on our horses.

For the safety of the group, it might be necessary to leave it if your horse acts up.

A gorgeous day, spectacular scenery and the company of compadres – it just doesn't get any better than this.

Mission Complete

Trail riding has been a way of life for me, and, I think you'll agree, after reading this book, that it's certainly been my passion. Over the years and many miles on my horse, I've often wondered how I could share my adventures with others, in hopes that some of their dreams and ambitions might become reality.

That's how this book came about, and it's been a labor of love for me. I hope you've learned from my experiences and that they spark some enthusiasm within you to enjoy your equine partner on the trail. Perhaps the photos, the how-to's and the stories will inspire you to fulfill your own trail riding dreams. If they do, then I've succeeded in my life's mission.

May all your trail rides be safe and happy ones.

PROFILE:
JANINE M. WILDER

Janine was born and raised in Athens County, Ohio, deep in the coal country of the Appalachian foothills. She, her three brothers and their parents lived as other coal mining families did at that time. Their four-room tarpaper home had no indoor plumbing, no telephone, nor any other modern convenience. They had no automobile, and horses, mules and ponies were used for only work in the mines, not for pleasure riding or transportation. The Thomas children walked wherever they needed to go.

After moving to Maryland as a young woman, she met and married her husband, Jim Wilder. They have five children and nine grandchildren. Janine attended college while she managed a family and numerous part-time jobs and graduated with high honors. Her education in ceramic engineering led to the high-tech cement research and development field, where she produced numerous patented matrixes and authored several scientific papers. The analytical skills she used to develop new products and to solve problems earned her awards and the respect of her colleagues and collaborators.

Later, in a career change, she developed her technical writing skills to fit the equine print and online media. Her articles have been published in many trail riding and horse magazines, both national and international. Janine's award-winning photography has appeared in numerous magazine articles, books, Web sites and advertising. She wrote, edited and produced her own newsletter, Horse Travels, for five years and continues to design and manage her own Web site, www.horsetravels.com.

Janine and Jim are members and the designated United States Experts of the Long Riders Guild, an exclusive society of equestrian explorers and adventurers.

Trail riding has been the Wilders' passion for the past 20 years, and traveling around the country with their horses has been their life's mission. These dedicated trail riders spent five years living on the road after selling their home and storing their belongings. Living in a motor home for five years taught them a lot about life, themselves and the beautiful country they live in.

Life is definitely the best teacher, and the knowledge from tens of thousands of miles on the road and on the trail has certainly been a life-changing adventure for Janine. She has ridden in all 48 contiguous states, Hawaii and the Yucatan jungle, and she continues her quest to find new and exciting places to ride. National, regional, state, county lands and parks and private facilities have hosted Janine and Jim along their way. Mountains, deserts, hill country, the plains and ocean beaches have exposed the Wilders and their horses to the many different facets of trail riding.

Because of her analytical abilities and well over 100,000 trail miles to draw from, Janine has a wealth of information and extraordinary experiences to share. Her love affair with trail horses began later in life than most trail riders, but her hours and years in the saddle have certainly made up for lost time, if not taken her past her peers in the trail riding field.

Janine, along with Jim, gives trail riding clinics and is a sought-after lecturer as she continues to see the country from the back of her horse.

Books Published by
WESTERN HORSEMAN®

ARABIAN LEGENDS by Marian K. Carpenter
280 pages and 319 photographs. Abu Farwa, *Aladdinn, *Ansata Ibn Halima, *Bask, Bay-Abi, Bay El Bey, Bint Sahara, Fadjur, Ferzon, Indraff, Khemosabi, *Morafic, *Muscat, *Naborr, *Padron, *Raffles, *Raseyn, *Sakr, Samtyr, *Sanacht, *Serafix, Skorage, *Witez II, Xenophonn.

BACON & BEANS, by Stella Hughes
144 pages and 200-plus recipes for delicious western chow.

BARREL RACING, Completely Revised by Sharon Camarillo
128 pages, 158 photographs and 17 illustrations. Teaches foundation horsemanship and barrel racing skills for horse and rider, with additional tips on feeding, hauling and winning.

CALF ROPING by Roy Cooper
144 pages and 280 photographs. Complete coverage of roping and tying.

CHARMAYNE JAMES ON BARREL RACING
by Charmayne James with Cheryl Magoteaux
192 pages and over 200 color photograps. Charmayne shares the training techniques and philosophy that made her the most successful barrel racer in history. Also included are vignettes of horses and riders that illustrate Charmayne's approach to indentifying and correcting problems in barrel racing, as well as examples and experiences from over 20 years as a world-class competitor in this exciting event.

COWBOYS & BUCKAROOS by Tim O'Byrne
176 pages and over 250 color photograps. The author, who's spent 20 years on ranches and feedyards, explains in great detail the trade secrets and working lifestyle of this North American icon. Readers can follow the cowboy crew through the four seasons of a cattle-industry year, learn their lingo and the Cowboy Code they live by, understand how they start colts, handle cattle, make long circles in rough terrain and much, much more. Many interesting sidebars, including excerpts from the author's personal journal offering firsthand accounts of the cowboy way.

CUTTING by Leon Harrel
144 pages and 200 photographs. Complete guide to this popular sport.

FIRST HORSE by Fran Devereux Smith
176 pages, 160 black-and-white photos, numerous illustrations. Step-by-step information for the first-time horse owner and/or novice rider.

HELPFUL HINTS FOR HORSEMEN
128 pages and 325 photographs and illustrations. WH readers and editors provide tips on every facet of life with horses and offer solutions to common problems horse owners share. Chapters include: Equine Health Care; Saddles; Bits and Bridles; Gear; Knots; Trailers/Hauling Horses; Trail Riding/Backcountry Camping; Barn Equipment; Watering Systems; Pasture, Corral and Arena Equipment; Fencing and Gates; Odds and Ends.

IMPRINT TRAINING by Robert M. Miller, D.V.M.
144 pages and 250 photographs. Learn to "program" newborn foals.

LEGENDS 1 by Diane Ciarloni
168 pages and 214 photographs. Barbra B, Bert, Chicaro Bill, Cowboy P-12, Depth Charge (TB), Doc Bar, Go Man Go, Hard Twist, Hollywood Gold, Joe Hancock, Joe Reed P-3, Joe Reed II, King P-234, King Fritz, Leo, Peppy, Plaudit, Poco Bueno, Poco Tivio, Queenie, Quick M Silver, Shue Fly, Star Duster, Three Bars (TB), Top Deck (TB) and Wimpy P-1.

LEGENDS 2 by Jim Goodhue, Frank Holmes, Phil Livingston, Diane Ciarloni
192 pages and 224 photographs. Clabber, Driftwood, Easy Jet, Grey Badger II, Jessie James, Jet Deck, Joe Bailey P-4 (Gonzales), Joe Bailey (Weatherford), King's Pistol, Lena's Bar, Lightning Bar, Lucky Blanton, Midnight, Midnight Jr, Moon Deck, My Texas Dandy, Oklahoma Star, Oklahoma Star Jr., Peter McCue, Rocket Bar (TB), Skipper W, Sugar Bars and Traveler.

LEGENDS 3 by Jim Goodhue, Frank Holmes, Diane Ciarloni, Kim Guenther, Larry Thornton, Betsy Lynch
208 pages and 196 photographs. Flying Bob, Hollywood Jac 86, Jackstraw (TB), Maddon's Bright Eyes, Mr Gun Smoke, Old Sorrel, Piggin String (TB), Poco Lena, Poco Pine, Poco Dell, Question Mark, Quo Vadis, Royal King, Showdown, Steel Dust and Two Eyed Jack.

LEGENDS 4
216 pages and 216 photographs. Several authors chronicle the great Quarter Horses Zantanon, Ed Echols, Zan Parr Bar, Blondy's Dude, Diamonds Sparkle, Woven Web/Miss Princess, Miss Bank, Rebel Cause, Tonto Bars Hank, Harlan, Lady Bug's Moon, Dash For Cash, Vandy, Impressive, Fillinic, Zippo Pine Bar and Doc O' Lena.

LEGENDS 5 by Frank Holmes, Ty Wyant, Alan Gold, Sally Harrison
248 pages, including about 300 photographs. The stories of Little Joe, Joe Moore, Monita, Bill Cody, Joe Cody, Topsail Cody, Pretty Buck, Pat Star Jr., Skipa Star, Hank H, Chubby, Bartender, Leo San, Custus Rastus (TB), Jaguar, Jackie Bee, Chicado V and Mr Bar None.

LEGENDS 6 by Frank Holmes, Patricia Campbell, Sally Harrison, GloryAnn Kurtz, Cheryl Magoteaux, Heidi Nyland, Bev Pechan, Juli S. Thorson
236 pages, including about 270 photographs. The stories of Paul A, Croton Oil, Okie Leo Flit Bar, Billietta, Coy's Bonanza, Major Bonanza, Doc Quixote, Doc's Prescription, Jewels Leo Bar, Colonel Freckles, Freckles Playboy, Peppy San, Mr San Peppy, Great Pine, The Invester, Speedy Glow, Conclusive, Dynamic Deluxe and Caseys Charm

NATURAL HORSE-MAN-SHIP by Pat Parelli
224 pages and 275 photographs. Parelli's six keys to a natural horse-human relationship.

PROBLEM-SOLVING, Volume 1 by Marty Marten
248 pages and over 250 photos and illustrations. Develop a willing partnership between horse and human — trailer-loading, hard-to-catch, barn-sour, spooking, water-crossing, herdbound and pull-back problems.

PROBLEM-SOLVING, Volume 2 by Marty Marten
A continuation of Volume 1. Ten chapters with illustrations and photos.

RAISE YOUR HAND IF YOU LOVE HORSES by Pat Parelli w. Kathy Swan
224 pages and over 200 black and white and color photos. The autobiography of the world's foremost proponent of natural horsemanship. Chapters contain hundreds of Pat Parelli stories, from the clinician's earliest remembrances to the fabulous experiences and opportunities he has enjoyed in the last decade. As a bonus, there are anecdotes in which Pat's friends tell stories about him.

RANCH HORSEMANSHIP by Curt Pate w. Fran Devereux Smith
220 pages and over 250 full color photos and illustrations. Learn how almost any rider at almost any level of expertise can adapt ranch-horse-training techniques to help his mount become a safer more enjoyable ride. Curt's ideas help prepare rider and horse for whatever they might encounter in the round pen, arena, pasture and beyond.

REINING, Completely Revised by Al Dunning
216 pages and over 300 photographs. Complete how-to training for this exciting event.

RIDE SMART, by Craig Cameron w. Kathy Swan
224 pages and over 250 black and white and color photos. Under one title, Craig Cameron combines a look at horses as a species and how to develop a positive, partnering relationship with them, along with good, solid horsemanship skills that suit both novice and experienced riders. Topics include ground-handling techniques, hobble-breaking methods, colt-starting, high performance maneuvers and trailer-loading. Interesting sidebars, such as trouble-shooting tips and personal anecdotes about Cameron's life, complement the main text.

RODEO LEGENDS by Gavin Ehringer
Photos and life stories fill 216 pages. Included are: Joe Alexander, Jake Barnes & Clay O'Brien Cooper, Joe Beaver, Leo Camarillo, Roy Cooper, Tom Ferguson, Bruce Ford, Marvin Garrett, Don Gay, Tuff Hedeman, Charmayne James, Bill Linderman, Larry Mahan, Ty Murray, Dean Oliver, Jim Shoulders, Casey Tibbs, Harry Tompkins and Fred Whitfield.

ROOFS AND RAILS by Gavin Ehringer
144 pages, 128 black-and-white photographs plus drawings, charts and floor plans. How to plan and build your ideal horse facility.

STARTING COLTS by Mike Kevil
168 pages and 400 photographs. Step-by-step process in starting colts.

THE HANK WIESCAMP STORY by Frank Holmes
208 pages and over 260 photographs. The biography of the legendary breeder of Quarter Horses, Appaloosas and Paints.

TEAM PENNING by Phil Livingston
144 pages and 200 photographs. How to compete in this popular family sport.

TEAM ROPING WITH JAKE AND CLAY by Fran Devereux Smith
224 pages and over 200 photographs and illustrations. Learn about fast times from champions Jake Barnes and Clay O'Brien Cooper. Solid information about handling a rope, roping dummies and heading and heeling for practice and in competition. Also sound advice about rope horses, roping steers, gear and horsemanship.

TRAIL RIDING by Janine M. Wilder
128 pages and over 150 color photographs. The author, who's ridden in all 48 states, Hawaii and the Yucatan over the last 20 years, has compiled a comprehensive guide that covers all the bases a trail rider needs in this fast-growing sport. She offers proven methods for developing a solid trail horse, safe ways to handle a variety of terrain, solutions for common trail problems, plus tips and resources on how to travel with horses. Interesting sidebars document her experiences on the trail.

WELL-SHOD by Don Baskins
160 pages, 300 black-and-white photos and illustrations. A horse-shoeing guide for owners and farriers. Easy-to-read, step-by-step how to trim and shoe a horse for a variety of uses. Special attention is paid to corrective shoeing for horses with various foot and leg problems.

WESTERN TRAINING by Jack Brainard
With Peter Phinny. 136 pages. Stresses the foundation for western training.

WIN WITH BOB AVILA by Juli S. Thorson
Hardbound, 128 full-color pages. Learn the traits that separate horse-world achievers from also-rans. World champion horseman Bob Avila shares his philosophies on succeeding as a competitor, breeder and trainer.

Western Horseman, established in 1936, is the world's leading horse publication. For subscription information: 800-877-5278.
To order other *Western Horseman* books: 800-874-6774 • *Western Horseman*, PO Box 470725, Fort Worth, TX 76147
Web site: **www.westernhorseman.com.**